oasis

(WHAT'S THE STORY) MORNING GLORY ?

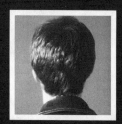

HAL•LEONARD CORPORATION

7777 W. BLUEMOUND RD. P.O. BOX 13819 MILWAUKEE, WI 53213

Exclusive Distributors:
Music Sales Limited
8/9 Frith Street, London W1V 5TZ, England.

Music Sales Pty Limited
120 Rothschild Avenue, Rosebery, NSW 2018, Australia.

Order No.AM934802
ISBN 0-7119-5465-8
This book © Copyright 1995 by Wise Publications.

Book design by Michael Bell Design.
Music arranged by Arthur Dick.
Music processed by The Pitts.

Printed in the United Kingdom by
Caligraving Limited, Thetford, Norfolk.

HELLO

I don't feel as if I know you
You take up all my time
The days are long and the night will throw you away
'Cause the sun don't shine

Nobody ever mentions the weather
Can make or break your day
Nobody ever seems to remember
Life is a game we play
We live in the shadows and we had the chance and threw it away

And it's never gonna be the same
'Cos the years are falling by the rain
It's never gonna be the same
'Til the light by you comes to my house and says hello

There ain't no sense in feeling lonely
They got no faith in you
But I've got a feeling you still owe me
So wipe the shit from your shoes

Nobody ever mentions the weather
Can make or break your day
Nobody ever seems to remember
Life is a game we play
We live in the shadows and we had the chance and threw it away

And it's never gonna be the same
'Cos the years are falling by the rain
It's never gonna be the same
'Til the light by you comes to my house and says

Hello, hello (it's good to be back, it's good to be back)
Hello, hello (it's good to be back, it's good to be back)
Hello, hello (it's good to be back, it's good to be back)
Hello, hello, hello

WONDERWALL

Today is gonna be the day
That they're gonna throw it back to you
By now you should have somehow
Realised what you gotta do
I don't believe that anybody feels the way that I do
About you now

Back beat, the word is on the street that the fire in your heart is out
I'm sure you've heard it all before but you never really had a doubt
I don't believe that anybody feels the way that I do about you now

And all the roads we have to walk are winding
And all the lights that lead us there are blinding
There are many things that I would like to say to you
But I don't know how

Because maybe you're gonna be the one that saves me
And after all you're my wonderwall

Today was gonna be the day
But they'll never throw it back to you
By now you should've somehow
Realised what you're not to do
I don't believe that anybody feels the way that I do
About you now

And all the roads that lead you there are winding
And all the lights that light the way are blinding
There are many things that I would like to say to you
But I don't know how

Because maybe you're gonna be the one that saves me
And after all you're my wonderwall

I said maybe you're gonna be the one that saves me
And after all you're my wonderwall

I said maybe you're gonna be the one that saves me
You're gonna be the one that saves me

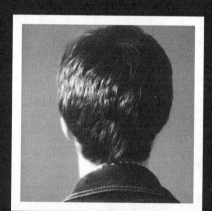

ROLL WITH IT

You gotta roll with it, you gotta take your time
You gotta say what you say, don't let anybody get in your way
'Cause it's all too much for me to take

Don't ever stand aside, don't ever be denied
You wanna be who you'd be if you're comin' with me
I think I've got a feelin' I've lost inside
I think I'm gonna take me away and hide
I'm thinkin' of things that I just can't abide

I know the roads down which your life will drive
I'll find the key that lets you stop inside
Kiss the girl she's not behind the door
But you know I think I recognise your face
But I never seen you before

You gotta roll with it, you gotta take your time
You gotta say what you say, don't let anybody get in your way
'Cause it's all too much for me to take

I know the roads down which your life will drive
I'll find the key that lets you stop inside
Kiss the girl she's not behind the door
But you know I think I recognise your face
But I never seen you before

You gotta roll with it, you gotta take your time
You gotta say what you say, don't let anybody get in your way
'Cause it's all too much for me to take

Don't ever stand aside, don't ever be denied
You wanna be who you'd be if you're comin' with me
I think I've got a feelin' I've lost inside
I think I've got a feelin' I've lost inside

DON'T LOOK BACK IN ANGER

Slip inside the eye of your mind
Don't you know you might find a better place to play
You said that you never been
But all the things that you've seen slowly fade away

So I must start a revolution from my bed
'Cause you said the brains I had went to my head
Step outside, summertime's in bloom
Stand up beside the fireplace, take that look from off your face
You ain't ever gonna burn my heart out

And so Sally can wait, she knows it's too late
As we're walking on by
Her soul slides away,
But don't look back in anger, I heard you say

Take me to the place where you go
Where nobody knows if it's night or day
But please don't put your life in the hands
Of a rock'n'roll band who'll throw it all away

I'm gonna start a revolution from my bed
'Cause you said the brains I had went to my head
Step outside, 'cause summertime's in bloom
Stand up beside the fireplace, take that look from off your face
'Cause you ain't never gonna burn my heart out

And so Sally can wait, she knows it's too late
As we're walking on by
Her soul slides away,
But don't look back in anger, I heard you say

So Sally can wait, she knows it's too late
As we're walking on by
Her soul slides away,
But don't look back in anger, I heard you say

So Sally can wait, she knows it's too late
As we're walking on by
Her soul slides away,
But don't look back in anger,
Don't look back in anger I heard you say
It's not too late

HEY NOW

I hitched a ride with my soul by the side of the road
Just as the sky turned black
I took a walk with my fame down memory lane
I never did find my way back

You know that I gotta say time's slippin' away
What will it hold for me?
What am I gonna do while I'm lookin' at you?
You're standing ignoring me

I thought that I heard someone say now
There's no time for running away now
Hey now, hey now

Feel no shame
'Cause time's no chain
Feel no shame

The first thing I saw
As I walked through the door
Was a sign on the wall that read
It said you might never know
That I want you to know
What's written inside of your head

And time as it stands
Won't be held in my hands
Or living inside of my skin
And as it fell from the sky
I asked myself why
Can I never let anyone in?

I thought that I heard someone say now
There's no time for running away now
Hey now, hey now

Feel no shame
'Cause time's no chain
Feel no shame

Feel no shame
'Cause time's no chain
Feel no shame

I hitched a ride with my soul by the side of the road
Just as the sky turned black
I took a walk with my fame down memory lane
I never did find my way back

You know that I gotta say time's slippin' away
What will it hold for me?
What am I gonna do while I'm lookin' at you?
You're standing ignoring me

I thought that I heard someone say now
There's no time for running away now
Hey now, hey now, hey now
Hey now, hey now, hey now, hey now
Hey now, hey now, hey now
Feel no shame
'Cause time's no chain
Feel no shame
'Cause time's no chain

SOME MIGHT SAY

Some might say that sunshine follows thunder
Go and tell it to the man who cannot shine
Some might say that we should never ponder
On our thoughts today 'cause they hold sway over time

Some might say we will find a brighter day
Some might say we will find a brighter day

'Cause I've been standing at the station in need of education in the rain
You made no preparation for my reputation once again
The sink is full of fishes, she's got dirty dishes on the brain
It was overflowing gently, it's so elemen'try my friend

Some might say they don't believe in heaven
Go and tell it to the man who lives in hell
Some might say you get what you've been given
If you don't get yours I won't get mine as well

Some might say we will find a brighter day
Some might say we will find a brighter day

'Cause I've been standing at the station in need of education in the rain
You made no preparation for my reputation once again
The sink is full of fishes, she's got dirty dishes on the brain
And my dog's been itching, itching in the kitchen once again

Some might say, some might say
You know what some might say
You know what some might say

CAST NO SHADOW

Here's a thought for every man
Who tries to understand what is in his hands
He walks along the open road of love and life
Arriving if he can

Bound with all the weight of all the words he tried to say
Chained to all the places that he never wished to stay
Bound with all the weight of all the words he tried to say
As he faced the sun he cast no shadow

As they took his soul they stole his pride
As they took his soul they stole his pride
As they took his soul they stole his pride
As he faced the sun he cast no shadow

Here's a thought for every man
Who tries to understand what is in his hands
He walks along the open road of love and life
Arriving if he can

Bound with all the weight of all the words he tried to say
Chained to all the places that he never wished to stay
Bound with all the weight of all the words he tried to say
As he faced the sun he cast no shadow

As they took his soul they stole his pride
As they took his soul they stole his pride
As they took his soul they stole his pride
As they took his soul they stole his pride

As he faced the sun he cast no shadow
As he faced the sun he cast no shadow
As he faced the sun he cast no shadow

CHAMPAGNE SUPERNOVA

How many special people change?
How many lives are living strange?
Where were you while we were getting high?
Slowly walking down the hall, faster than a cannon ball
Where were you while we were getting high?
Some day you will find me caught beneath the landslide
In a Champagne Supernova in the sky
Some day you will find me caught beneath the landslide
In a Champagne Supernova, a Champagne Supernova in the sky

Wake up the dawn and ask her why
A dreamer dreams, she never dies
Wipe that tear away now from your eyes
Slowly walkin' down the hall, faster than a cannon ball
Where were you while we were getting high?

Some day you will find me caught beneath the landslide
In a Champagne Supernova in the sky
Some day you will find me caught beneath the landslide
In a Champagne Supernova, a Champagne Supernova

'Cause people believe that they're gonna get away from the summer
But you and I, we live and die
The world's still spinning round, we don't know why
Why, why, why, why

How many special people change?
How many lives are living strange?
Where were you while we were getting high?
Slowly walking down the hall, faster than a cannon ball
Where were you while we were getting high?

Some day you will find me caught beneath the landslide
In a Champagne Supernova in the sky
Some day you will find me caught beneath the landslide
In a Champagne Supernova, a Champagne Supernova

'Cause people believe that they're gonna get away from the summer
But you and I, we live and die
The world's still spinning round, we don't know why
Why, why, why, why

How many special people change?
How many lives are living strange?
Where were you when we were getting high?
We were getting high
We were getting high
We were getting high
We were getting high
We were getting high

SHE'S ELECTRIC

She's electric,
She's in a family full of eccentrics
She's done things I've never expected
And I need some time
She's got a sister
And God only knows how I've missed her
And on the palm of her hand is a blister
And I need more time

And I want you to know I've got my mind made up now
But I need more time

And I want you to say, do you know what I'm saying?
But I need more, 'cause I'll be you and you'll be me
There's lots and lots for us to see
Lots and lots for us to do
She is electric, can I be electric too?

She's got a brother
We don't get on with one another
But I quite fancy her mother
And I think that she likes me
She's got a cousin
In fact she's got 'bout a dozen
She's got one in the oven
But it's nothing to do with me

And I want you to know I've got my mind made up now
But I need more time

And I want you to say, do you know what I'm saying?
But I need more, 'cause I'll be you and you'll be me
There's lots and lots for us to see
Lots and lots for us to do
She is electric, can I be electric too?
Can I be electric too?
Can I be electric too?
Can I be electric too?

MORNING GLORY

All your dreams are made
When you're chained to the mirror with your razor blade
Today's the day that all the world will see
Another sunny afternoon
Walking to the sound of my favourite tune
Tomorrow never knows what it doesn't know too soon

Need a little time to wake up
Need a little time to wake up, wake up
Need a little time to wake up
Need a little time to rest your mind
You know you should, so I guess you might as well

What's the story, Morning Glory?
Well, you need a little time to wake up, wake up
Well, what's the story, Morning Glory?
Well, you need a little time to wake up, wake up

All your dreams are made
When you're chained to the mirror with your razor blade
Today's the day that all the world will see
Another sunny afternoon
Walking to the sound of my favourite tune
Tomorrow never knows what it doesn't know too soon

Need a little time to wake up
Need a little time to wake up, wake up
Need a little time to wake up
Need a little time to rest your mind
You know you should, so I guess you might as well

What's the story, Morning Glory?
Well, you need a little time to wake up, wake up
Well, what's the story, Morning Glory?
Well, you need a little time to wake up, wake up

Well, what's the story, Morning Glory?
Well, you need a little time to wake up, wake up
Well, what's the story, Morning Glory?
Well, you need a little time to wake up, wake up

Tablature & Instructions Explained

The tablature stave comprises six lines, each representing a string on the guitar as illustrated.

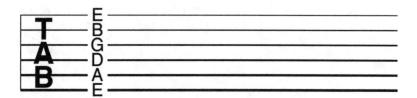

A number on any of the lines indicates, therefore, the string and fret on which a note should be played.

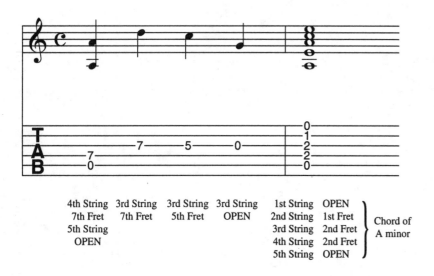

4th String	3rd String	3rd String	3rd String	1st String	OPEN	
7th Fret	7th Fret	5th Fret	OPEN	2nd String	1st Fret	Chord of
5th String				3rd String	2nd Fret	A minor
OPEN				4th String	2nd Fret	
				5th String	OPEN	

A useful hint to help you read tablature is to cut out small squares of self-adhesive paper and stick them on the upper edge of the guitar neck adjacent to each of the frets, numbering them accordingly. Be careful to use paper that will not damage the finish on your guitar.

Finger Vibrato

Tremolo Arm Vibrato

Glissando

Gliss

Strike the note, then slide the finger up or down the fretboard as indicated.

Tremolo Strumming

This sign indicates fast up and down stroke strumming.

8va

This sign indicates that the notes are to be played an octave higher than written.

loco

This instruction cancels the above.

This note-head indicates the string is to be totally muted to produce a percussive effect.

P.M. = Palm mute

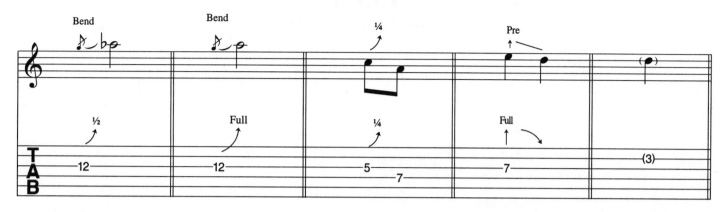

HALF TONE BEND

Play the note G then bend the string so that the pitch rises by a half tone (semi-tone).

FULL TONE BEND

DECORATIVE BEND

PRE-BEND

Bend the string as indicated, strike the string and release.

GHOST NOTE

The note is half sounded

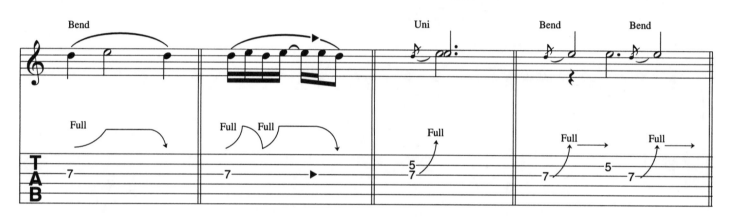

BEND & RELEASE

Strike the string, bend it as indicated, then release the bend whilst it is still sounding.

BEND & RESTRIKE

Strike the string, bend or gliss as indicated, then restrike the string where the symbol occurs.

UNISON BEND

Strike both strings simultaneously then immediately bend the lower string as indicated.

STAGGERED UNISON BEND

Strike the lower string and bend as indicated; whilst it is still sounding strike the higher string.

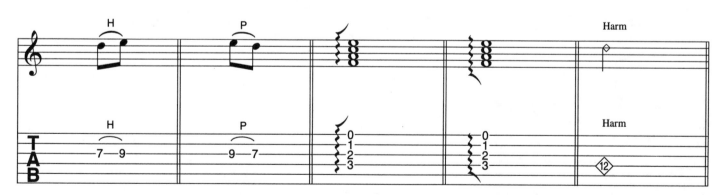

HAMMER-ON

Hammer a finger down on the next note without striking the string again.

PULL-OFF

Pull your finger off the string with a plucking motion to sound the next note without striking the string again.

RAKE-UP

Strum the notes upwards in the manner of an arpeggio.

RAKE-DOWN

Strum the notes downwards in the manner of an arpeggio.

HARMONICS

Strike the string whilst touching it lightly at the fret position shown. Artificial Harmonics, (A.H.), will be described in context.

Hello

Words & Music by Noel Gallagher

(includes extract from Hello, Hello, I'm Back Again - Words & Music by Gary Glitter & Mike Leander)

1. I don't feel as if I know you, you take up all my time. The
See Block Lyrics for Verse 2

days are long and the night will throw you a-way 'cause the sun don't shine.

No-bo-dy e-ver men-tions the weath-er can make or break__ your day._____

No-bo-dy e-ver seems__ to re-mem-ber life is a game__ we play.____

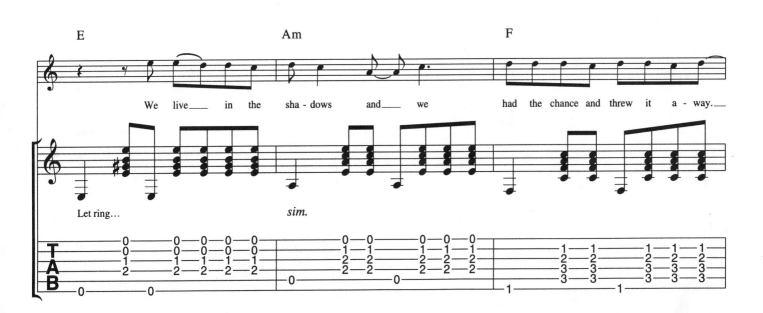

We live___ in the sha-dows and___ we had the chance and threw it a-way.__

Let ring…   sim.

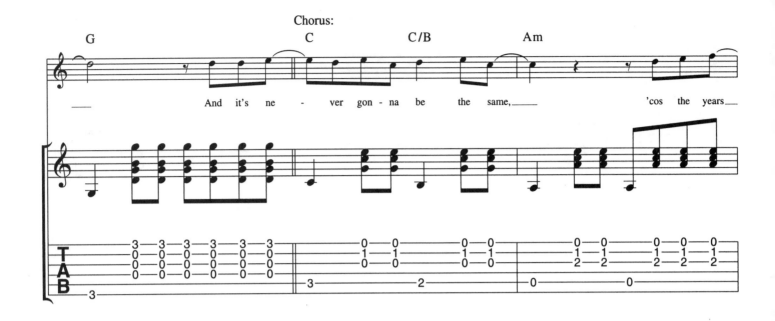

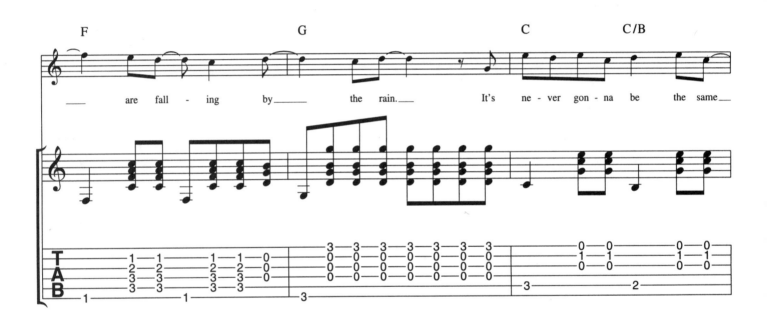

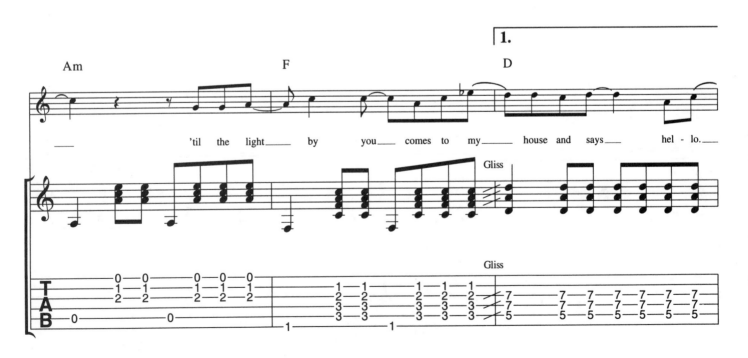

to begin.

2. There

2nd verse

2.

house and says:

Hel - lo,

hel - lo.

(It's good to be back, it's

Vocal tacet 2nd time

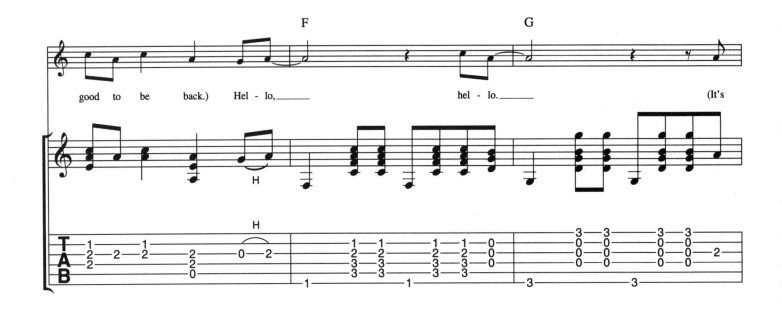

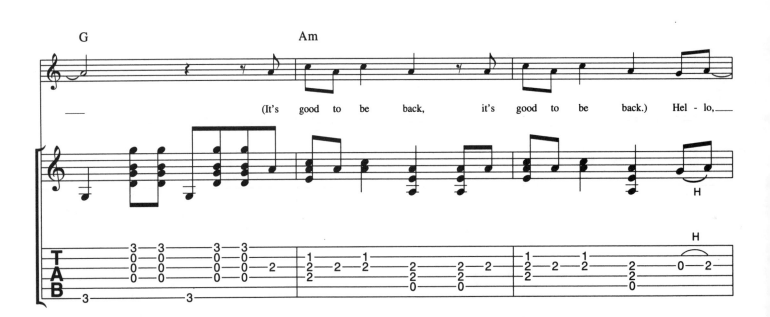

Verse 2:
There ain't no sense in feeling lonely
They got no faith in you
But I've got a feeling you still owe me
So wipe the shit from your shoes.

Nobody ever mentions the weather *etc…*

Roll With It

Words & Music by Noel Gallagher

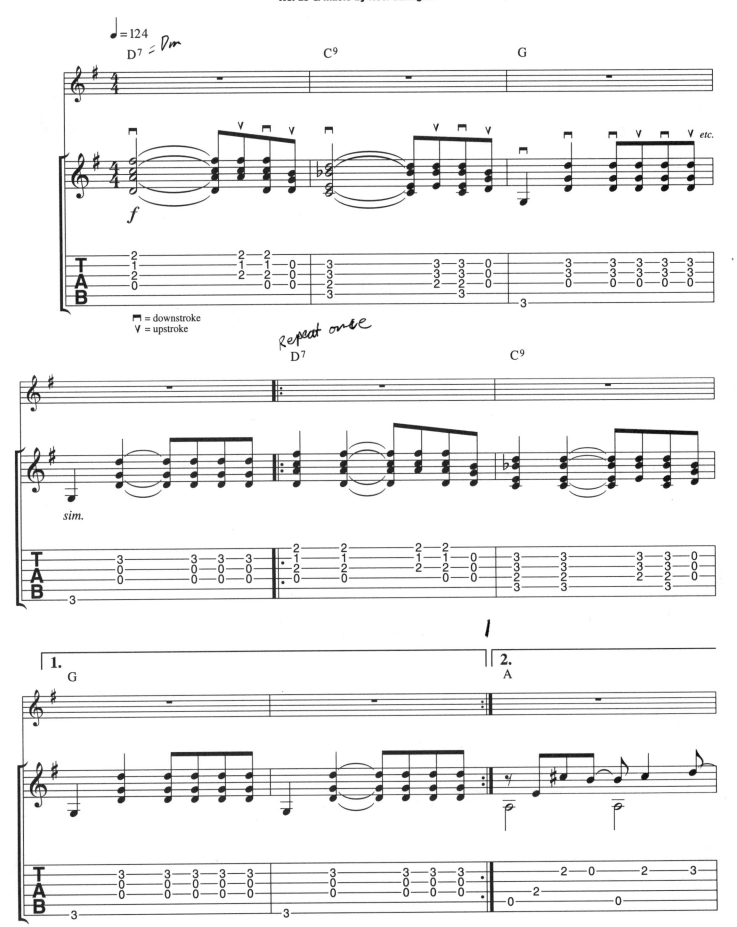

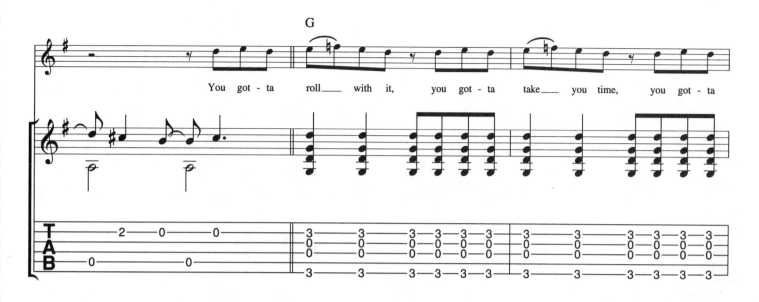

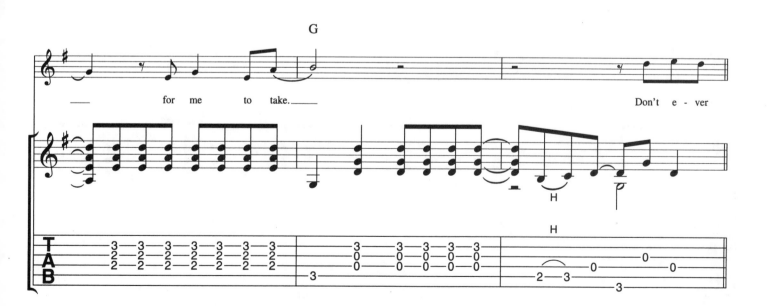

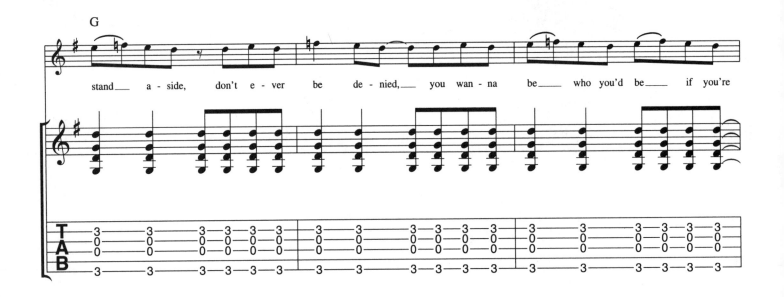

stand___ a - side, don't e - ver be de - nied,___ you wan - na be___ who you'd be___ if you're

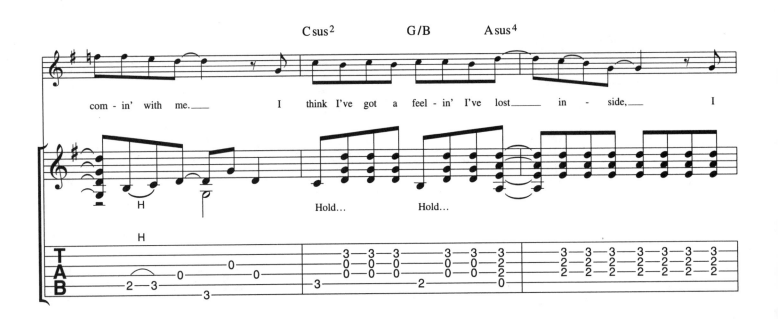

Csus² G/B Asus⁴

com - in' with me.___ I think I've got a feel - in' I've lost___ in - side,___ I

Hold... Hold...

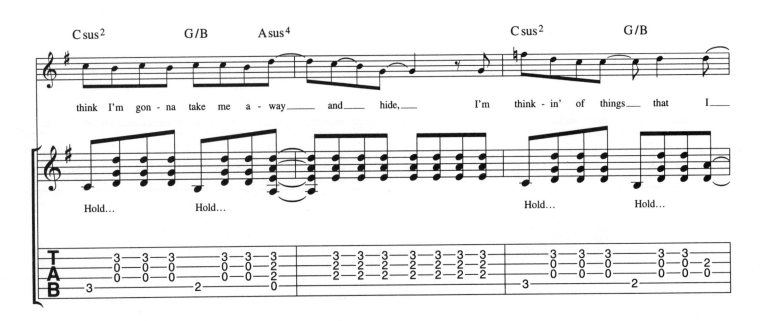

Csus² G/B Asus⁴ Csus² G/B

think I'm gon - na take me a - way___ and___ hide,___ I'm think - in' of things___ that I___

Hold... Hold... Hold... Hold...

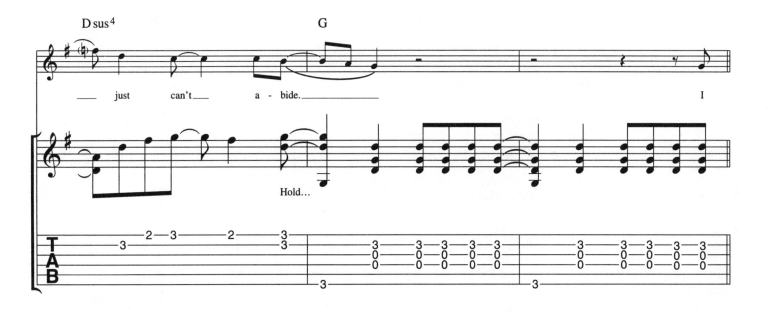

just can't a-bide.   I

Hold...

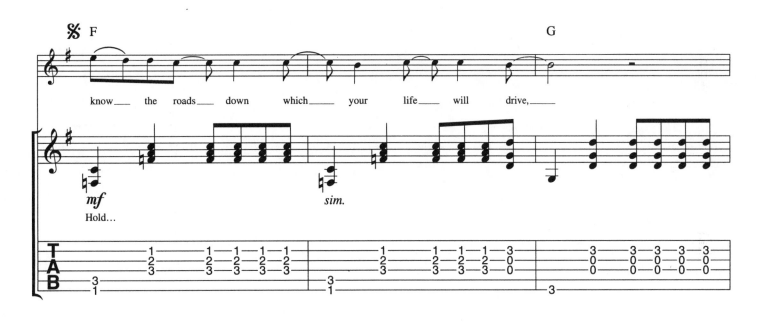

know the roads down which your life will drive,

Hold...
mf
sim.

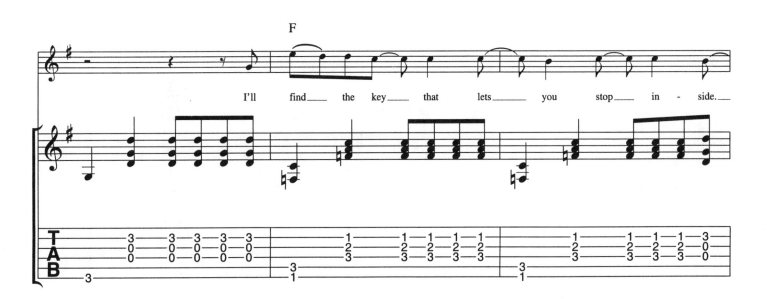

I'll find the key that lets you stop in-side.

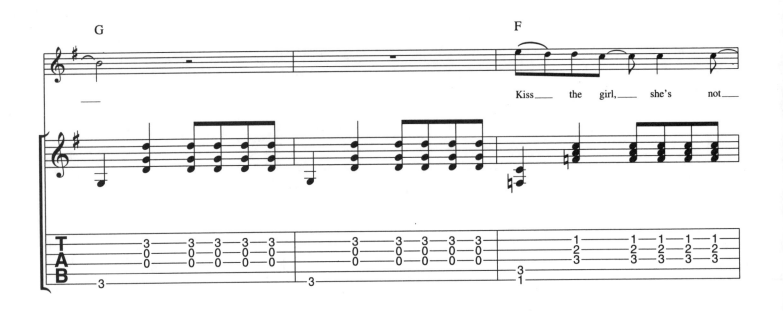

Kiss__ the girl,__ she's not__

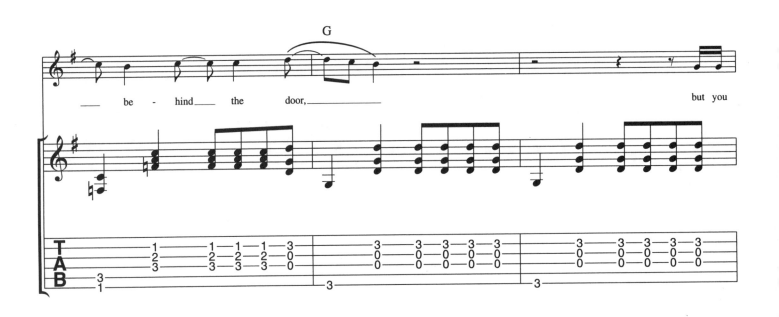

__ be - hind__ the door,_____ but you

know I think I rec - og - nise____ your face____ but I ne - ver seen you be - fore.___

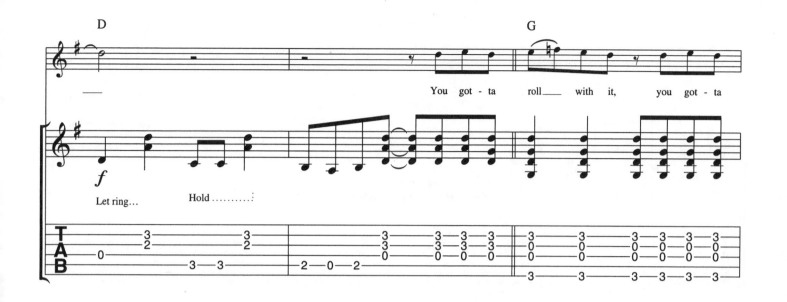

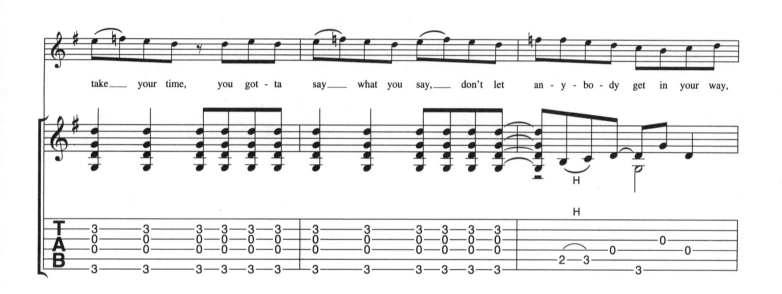

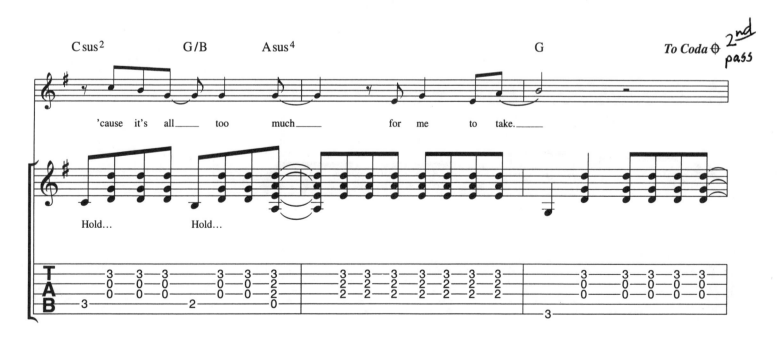

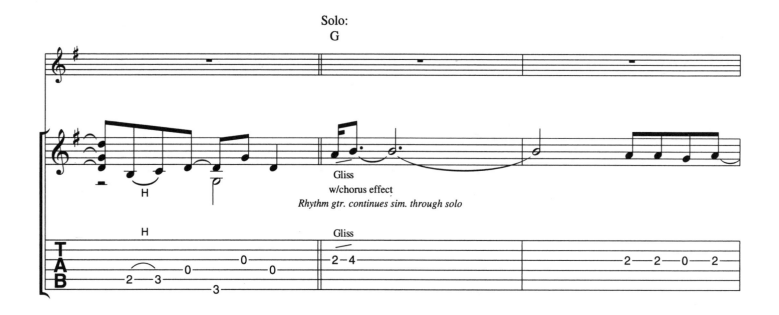

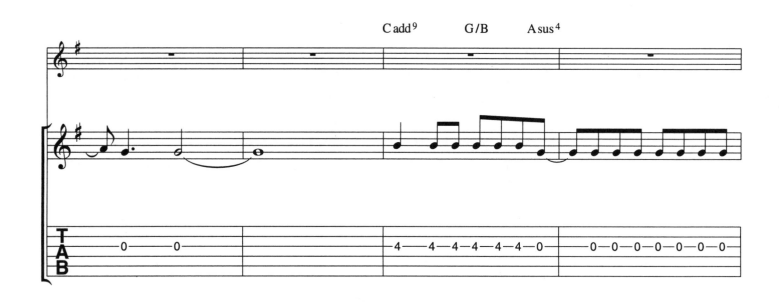

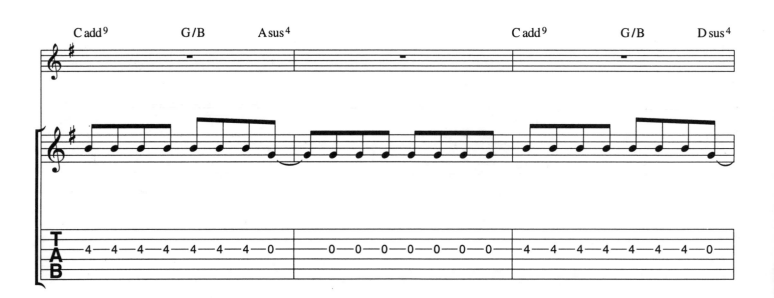

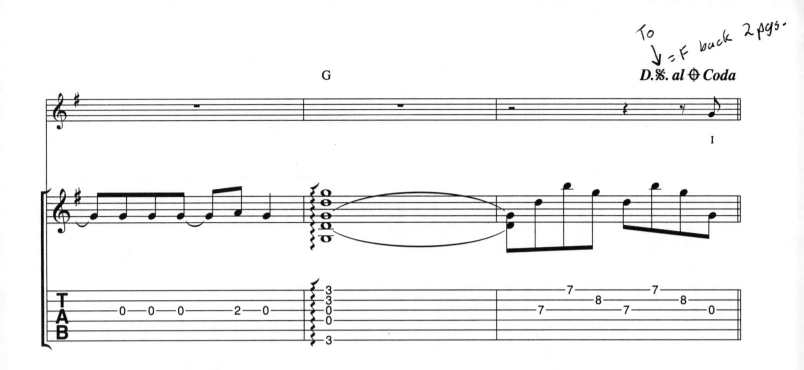

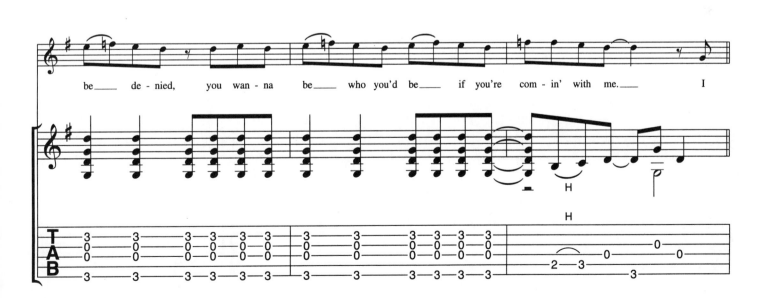

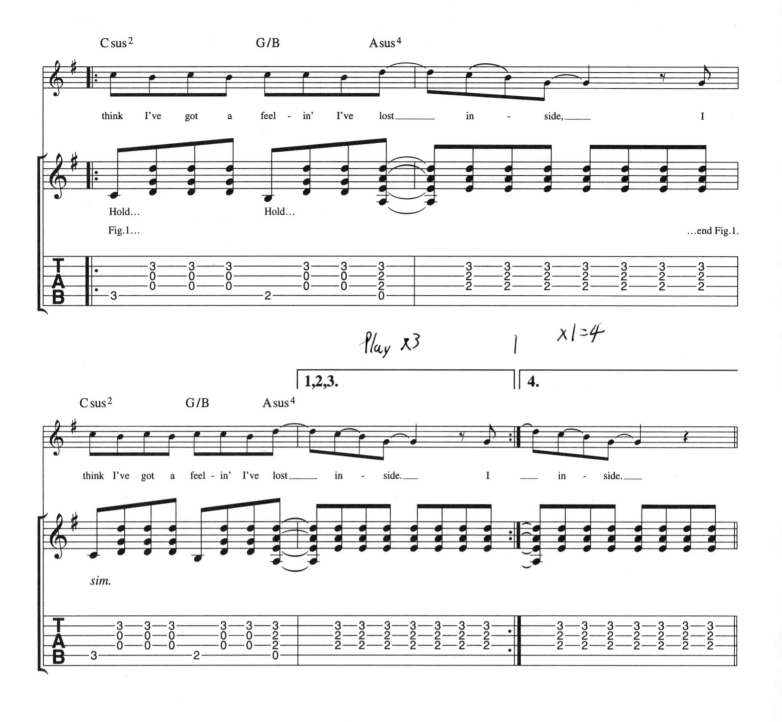

think I've got a feel - in' I've lost_____ in - side,_____ I

Hold… Hold…
Fig.1… …end Fig.1.

Play x3 | x1=4

1,2,3.   **4.**

think I've got a feel - in' I've lost_____ in - side._____ I _____ in - side._____

sim.

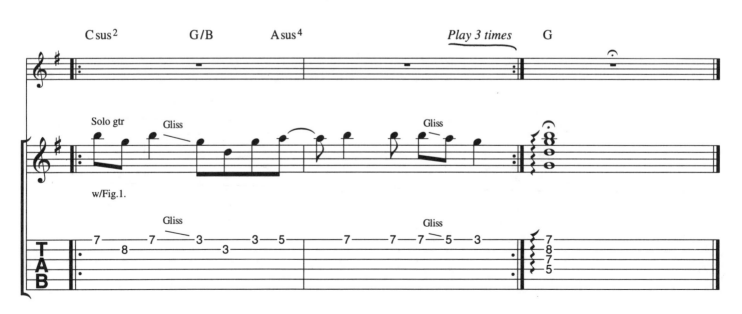

Solo gtr
w/Fig.1.

Play 3 times

Wonderwall

Words & Music by Noel Gallagher

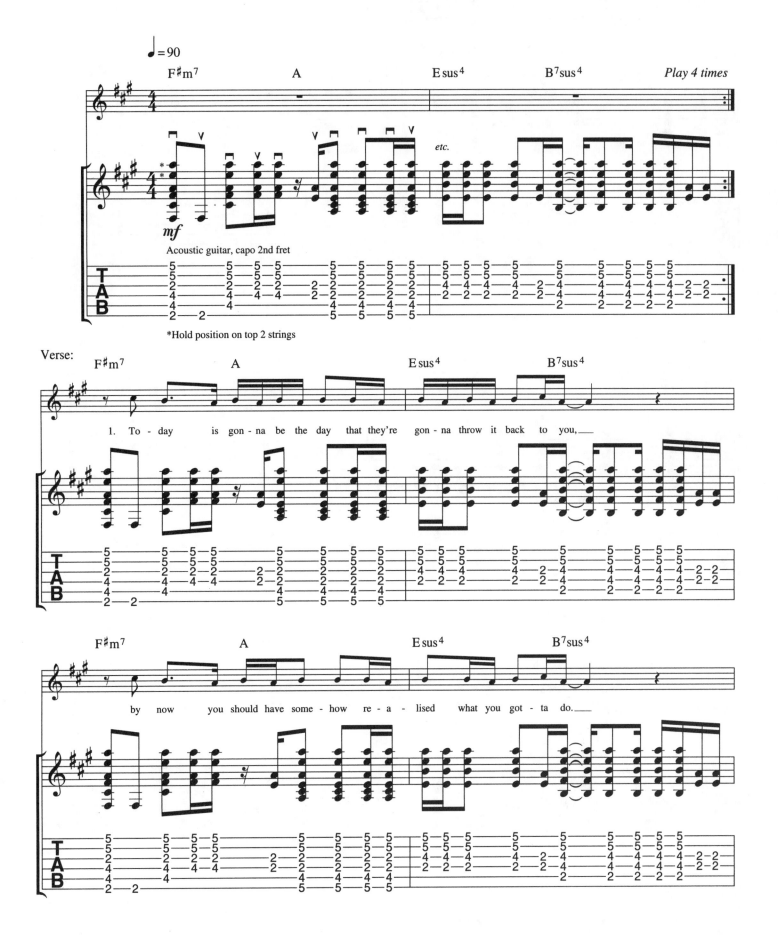

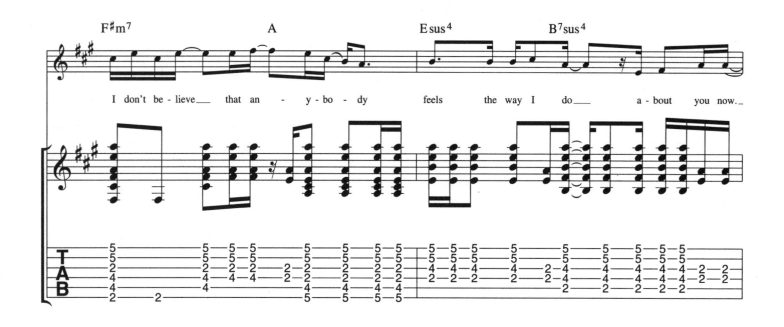

I don't be-lieve___ that an - y-bo - dy feels the way I do___ a-bout you now.

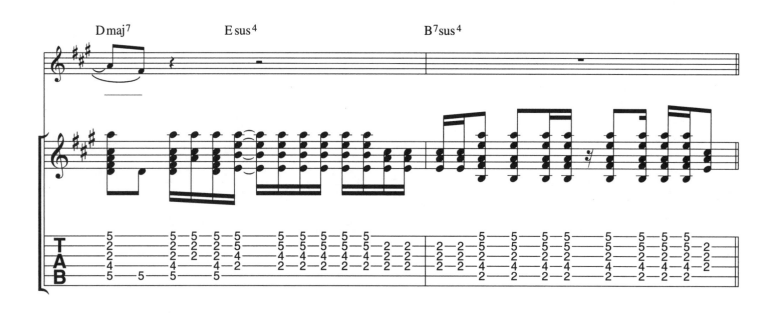

Verse :

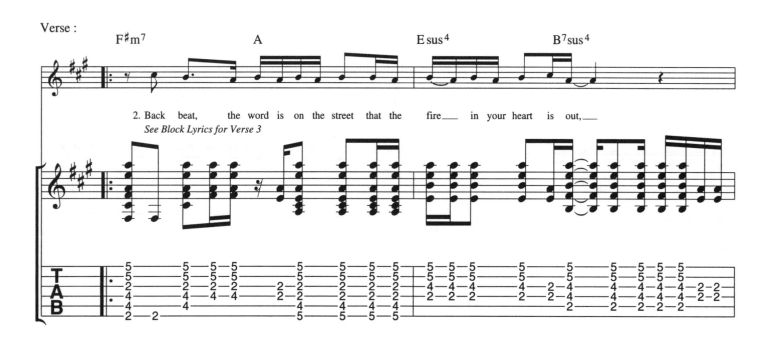

2. Back beat, the word is on the street that the fire___ in your heart is out,___
See Block Lyrics for Verse 3

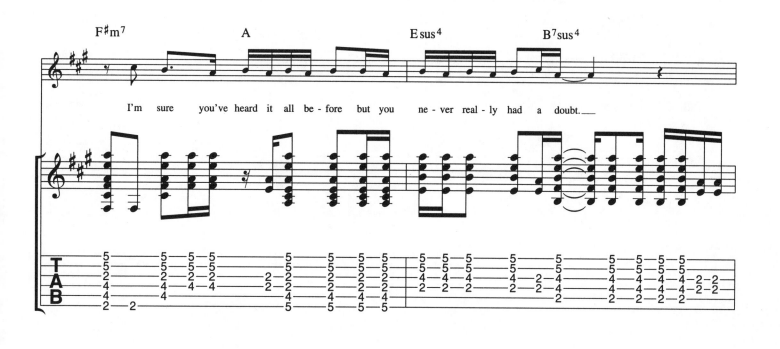

I'm sure you've heard it all be-fore but you ne-ver real-ly had a doubt.___

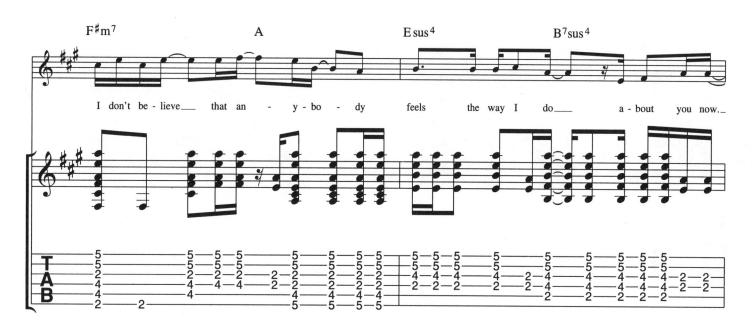

I don't be-lieve___ that an-y-bo-dy feels the way I do___ a-bout you now.___

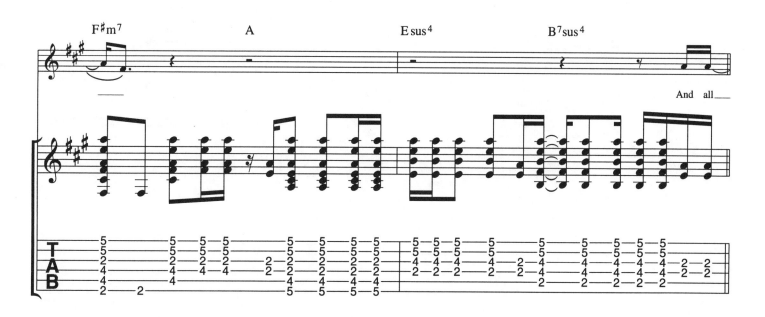

And all___

26

B^{7}sus^4

Be - cause

Chorus:

D add^9 F$^\sharp$m^7 A   F$^\sharp$m

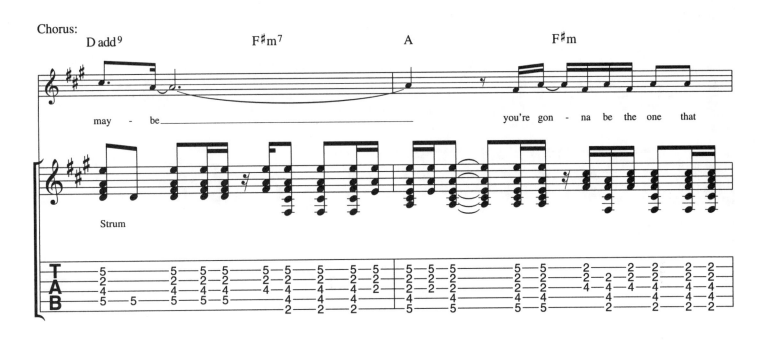

may - be _____ you're gon - na be the one that

Strum

D add^9 F$^\sharp$m   A   F$^\sharp$m

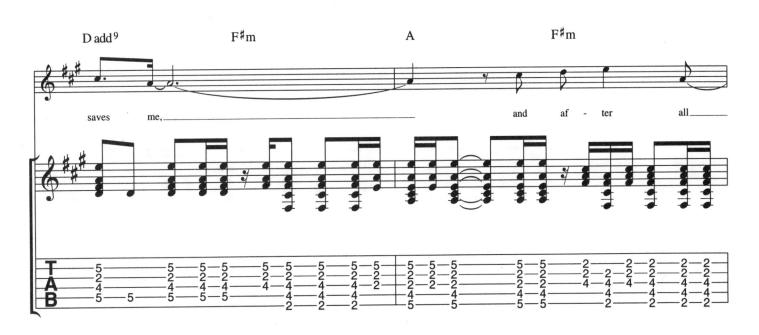

saves   me, _____ and af - ter all ___

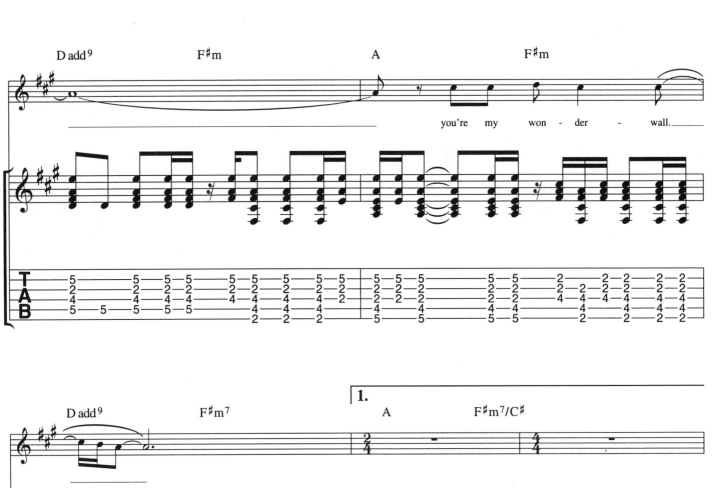

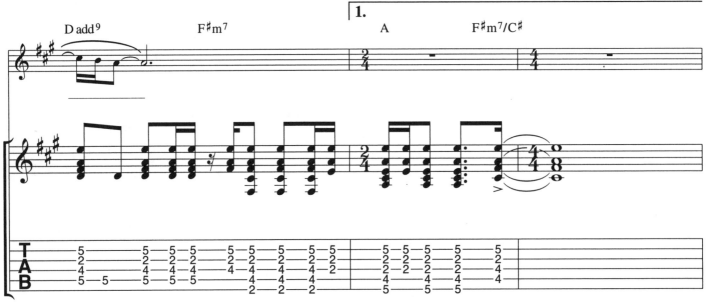

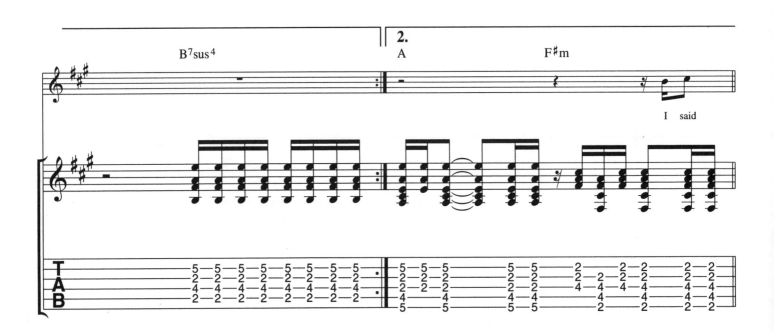

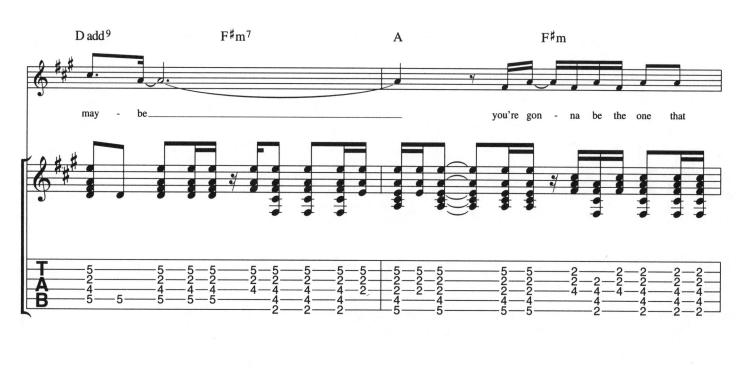

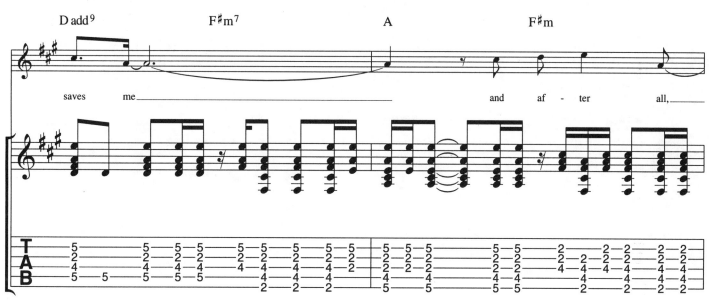

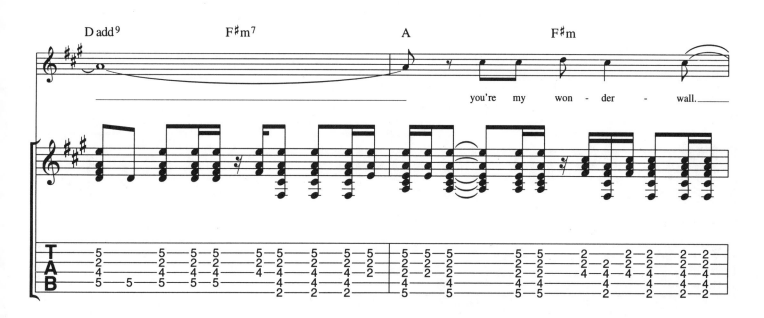

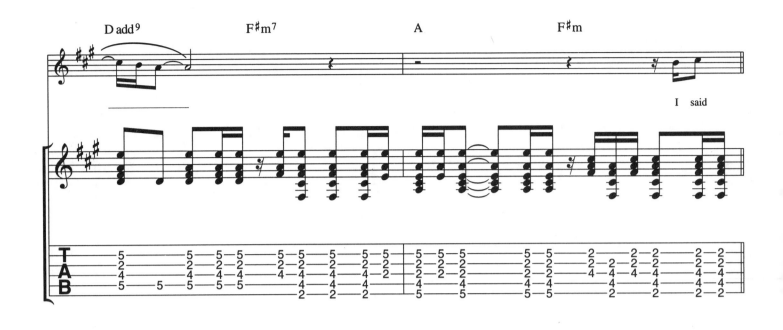

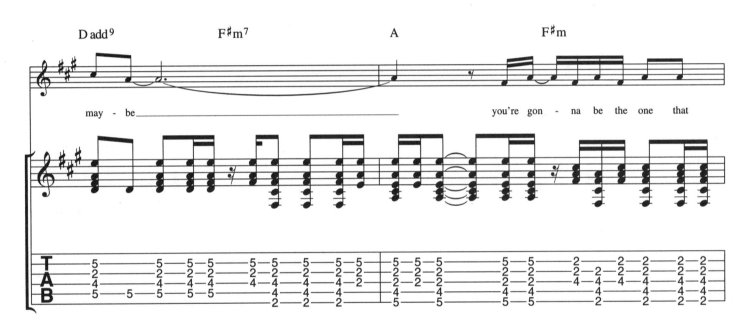

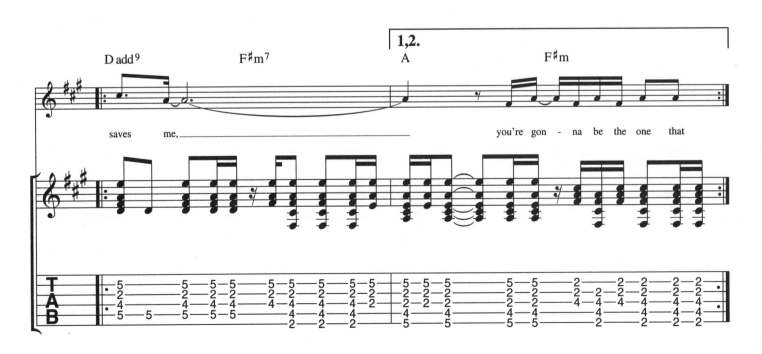

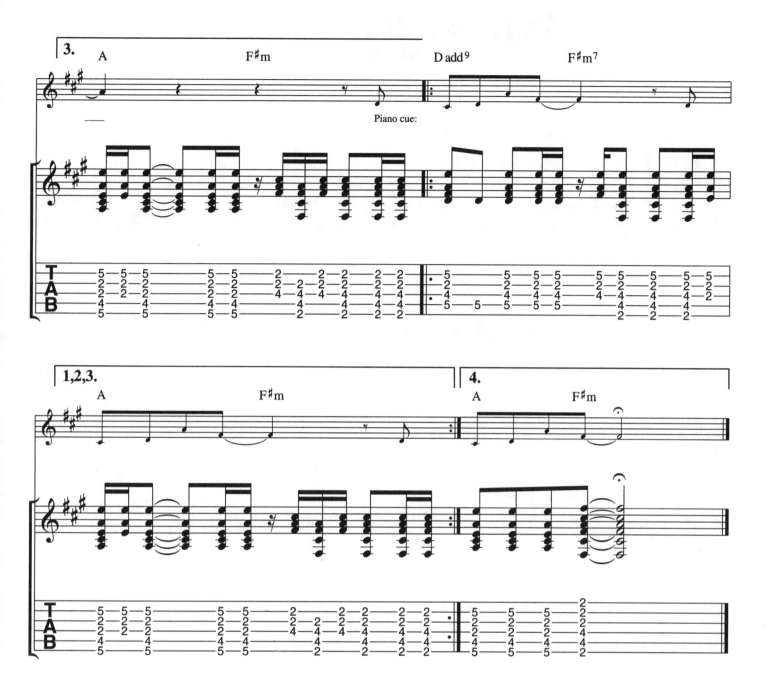

Verse 3:
Today was gonna be the day
But they'll never throw it back to you
By now you should've somehow
Realised what you're not to do
I don't believe that anybody feels the way I do
About you now.

And all the roads that lead you there were winding
And all the lights that light the way are blinding
There are many things that I would like to say to you
But I don't know how.

Don't Look Back In Anger

Words & Music by Noel Gallagher

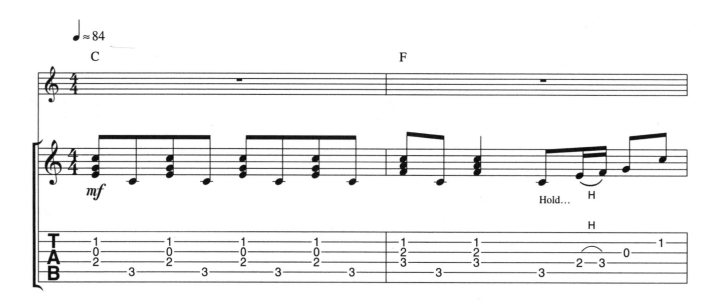

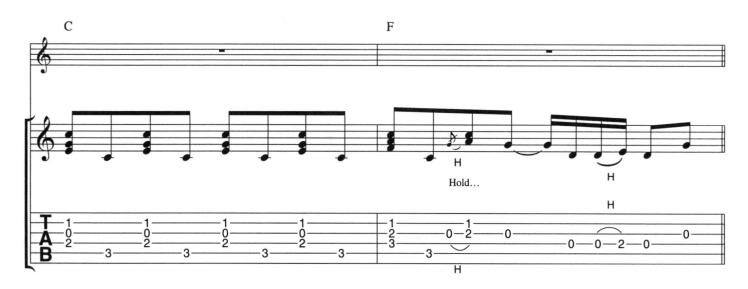

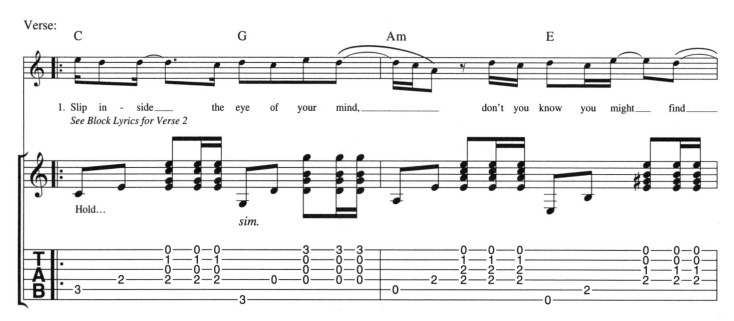

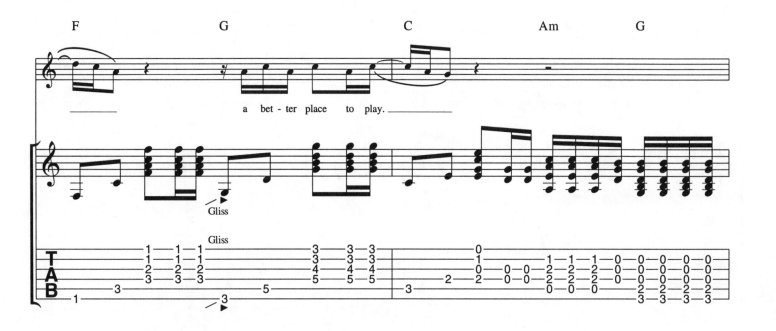

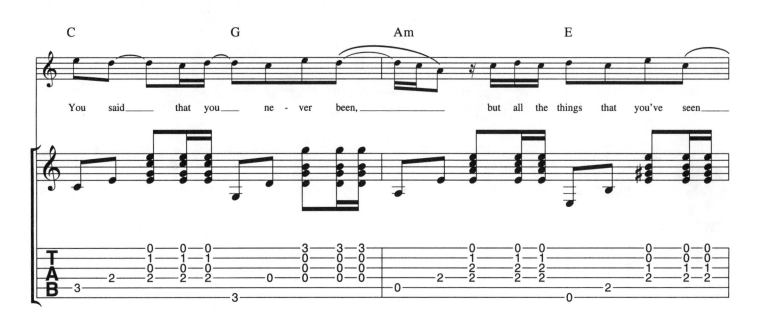

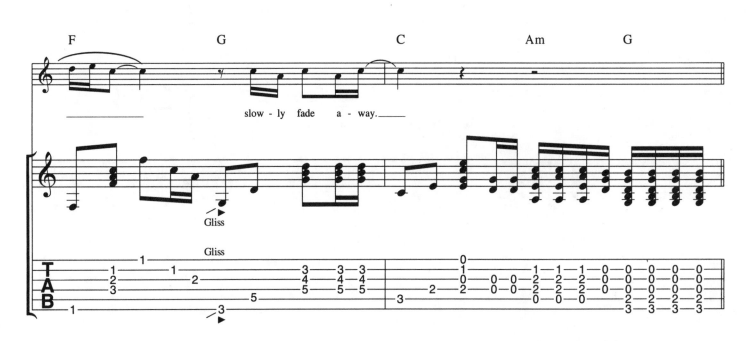

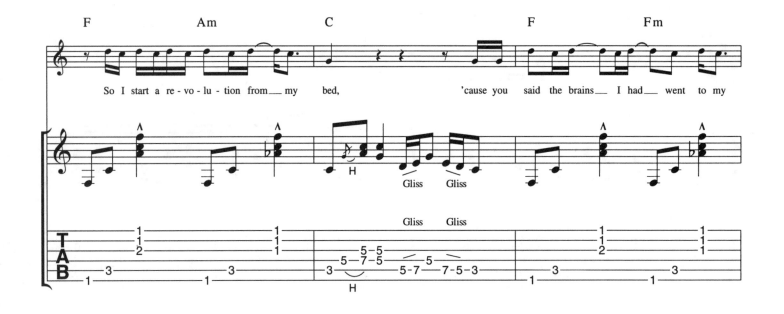

So I start a re-vo-lu-tion from my bed, 'cause you said the brains I had went to my

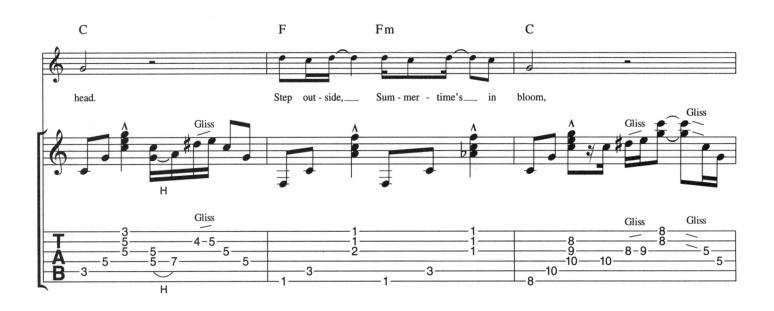

head. Step out-side, Sum-mer-time's in bloom,

stand up be-side the fire - place, take that look from off your face, you ain't e - ver gon - na burn my

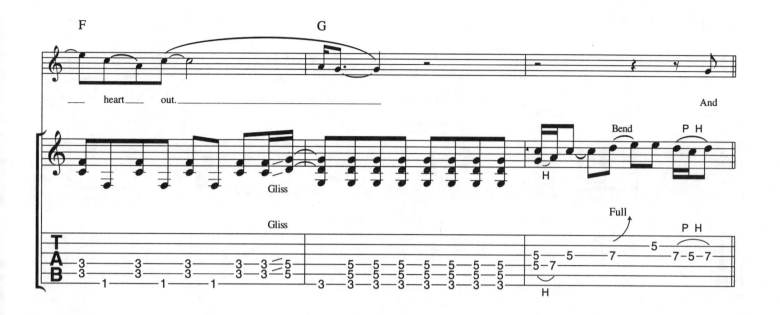

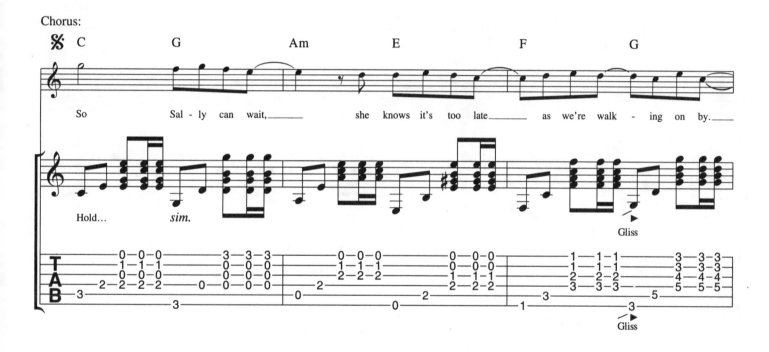

Chorus:

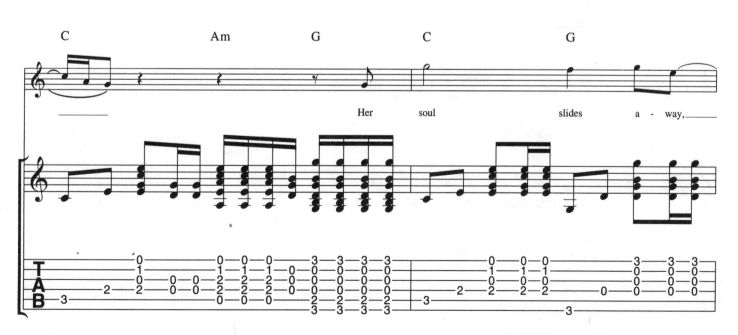

but don't____ look back____ in an - ger, I heard you say.___

To Coda ⊕

Gliss

Gliss

1.

Solo:

Rhythm gtr continues sim.

Bend

Full

Gliss

Gliss

Gliss

Gliss

to beginning

2.

H

H

H

H

Solo:

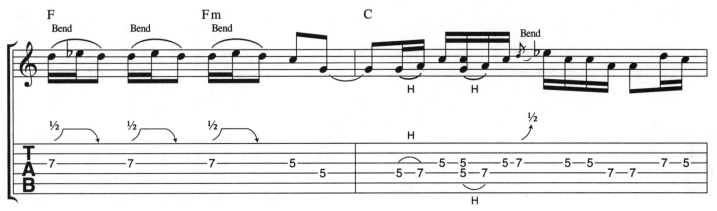

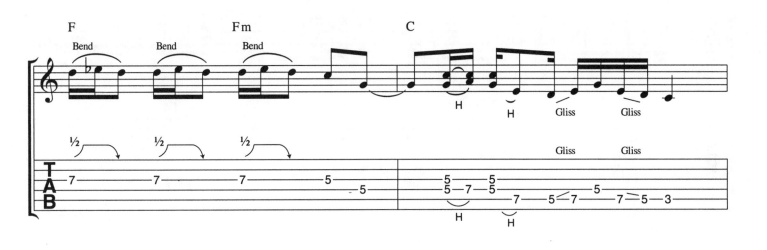

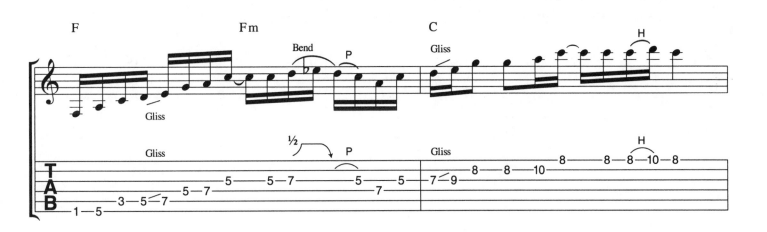

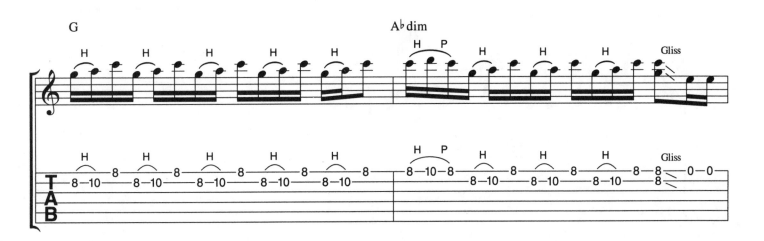

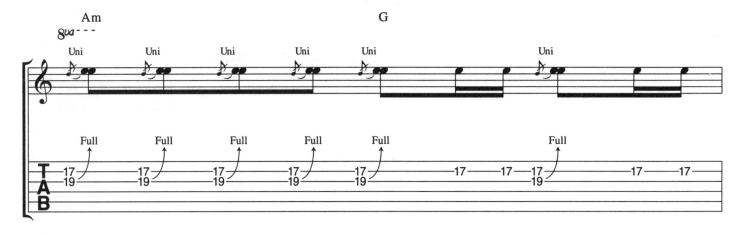

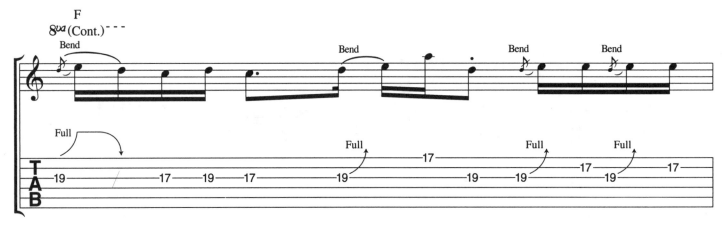

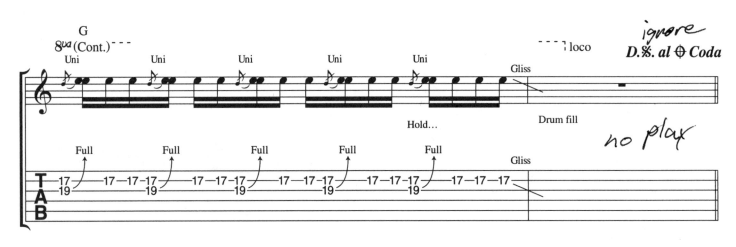

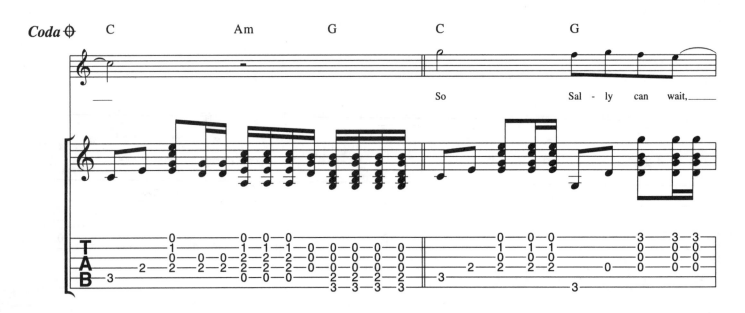

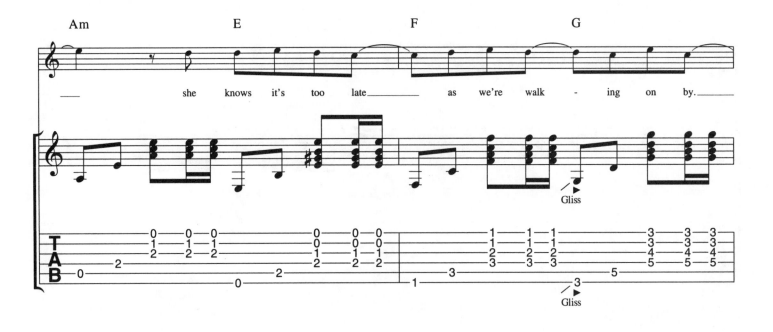

she knows it's too late_____ as we're walk - ing on by._____

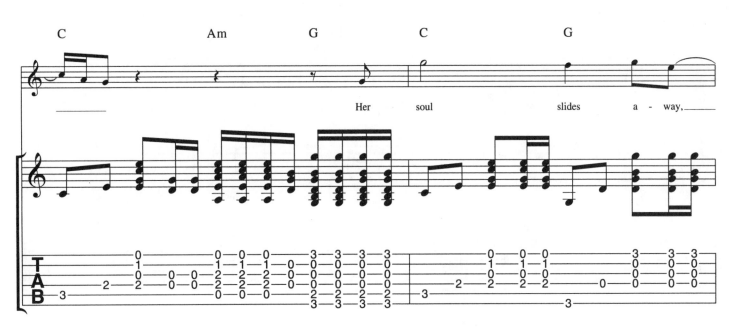

Her soul slides a - way,_____

but don't__ look back_____ in an - ger, don't look back in an - ger,_____

mp

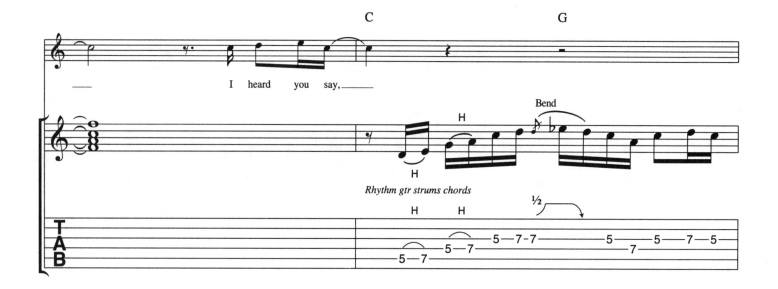

I heard you say,___

Rhythm gtr strums chords

it's not too late.

Verse 2:
Take me to the place where you go
Where nobody knows if it's night or day
But please don't put your life in the hands
Of a rock 'n' roll band who'll throw it all away.

I'm gonna start a revolution from my bed
'Cause you said the brains I had went to my head
Step outside 'cause summertime's in bloom
Stand up beside the fireplace, take that look from off your face
'Cause you ain't never gonna burn my heart out.

Cast No Shadow

Words & Music by Noel Gallagher

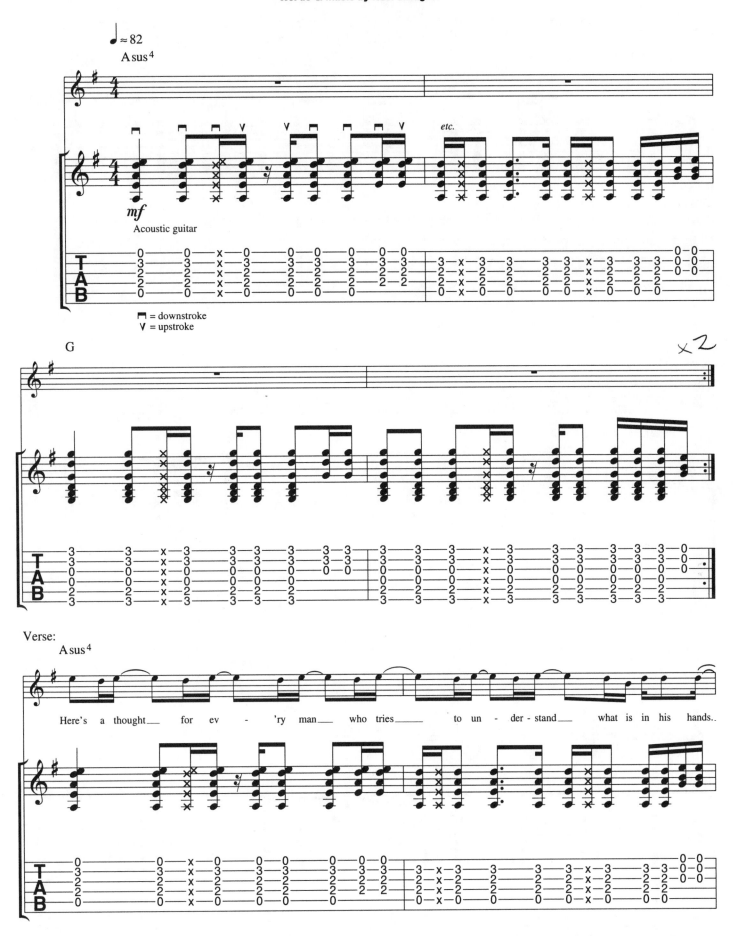

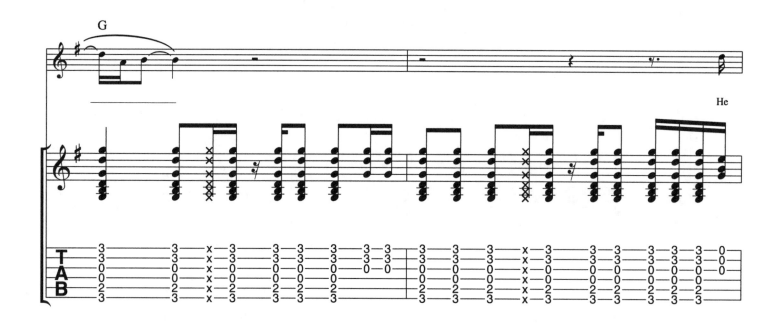

He

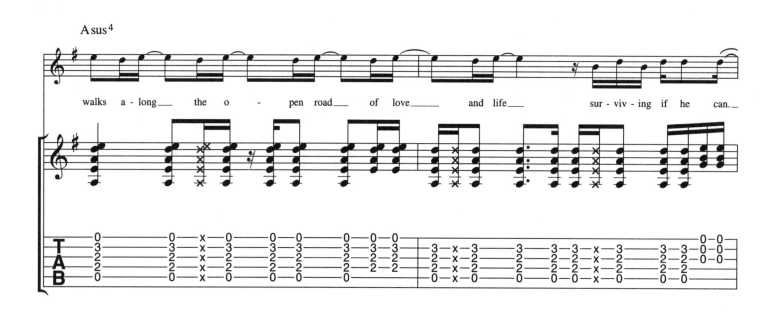

walks a - long___ the o - pen road___ of love___ and life___ sur - viv - ing if he can.___

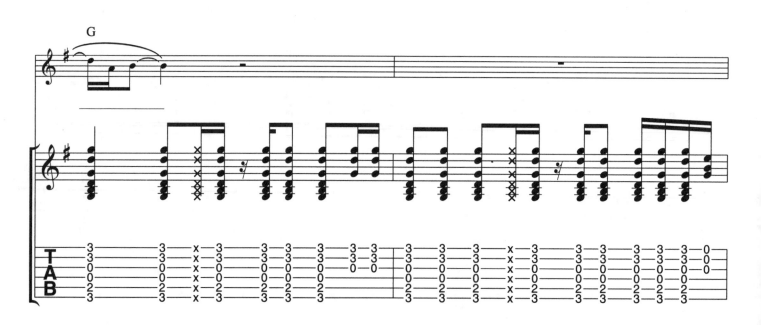

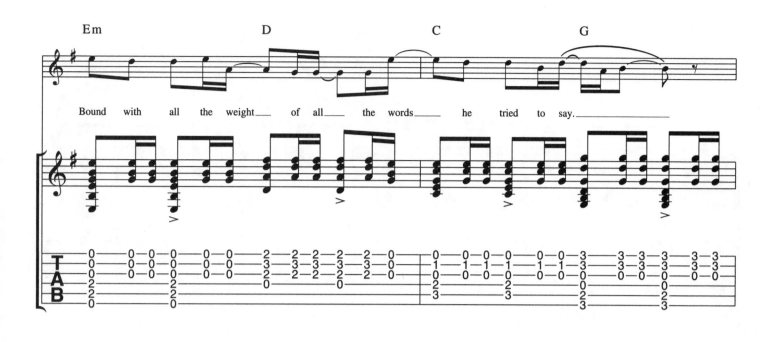

Bound with all the weight of all the words he tried to say.

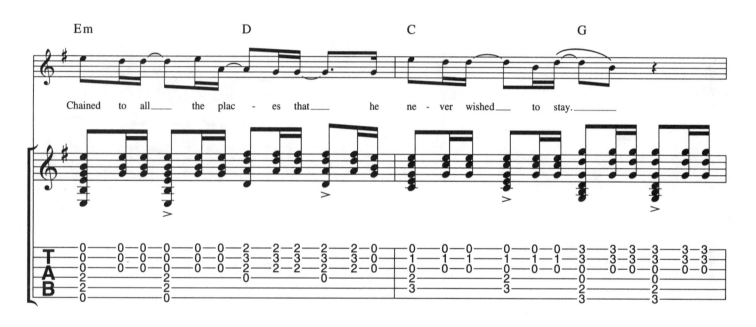

Chained to all the plac - es that he ne - ver wished to stay.

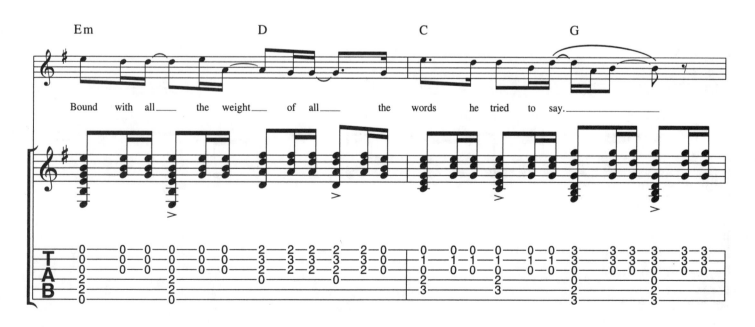

Bound with all the weight of all the words he tried to say.

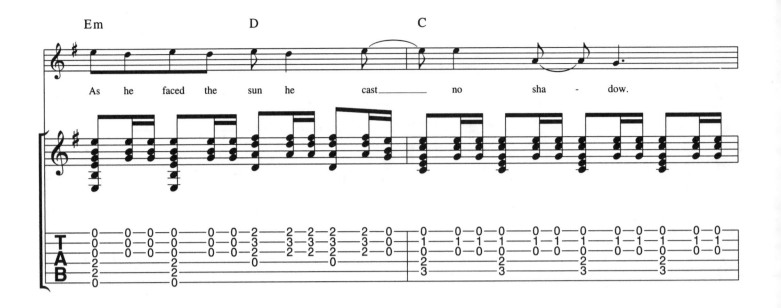

As he faced the sun he cast___ no sha - dow.

Chorus:

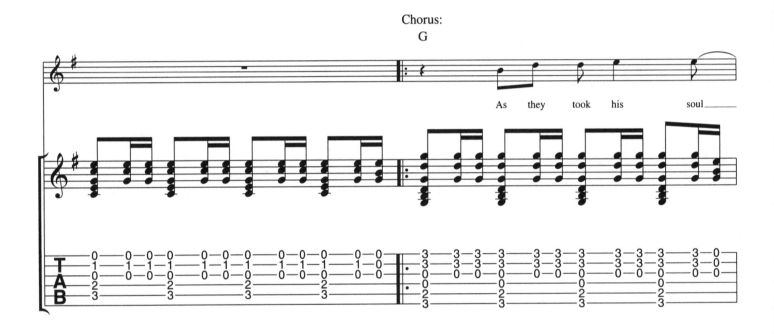

As they took his soul___

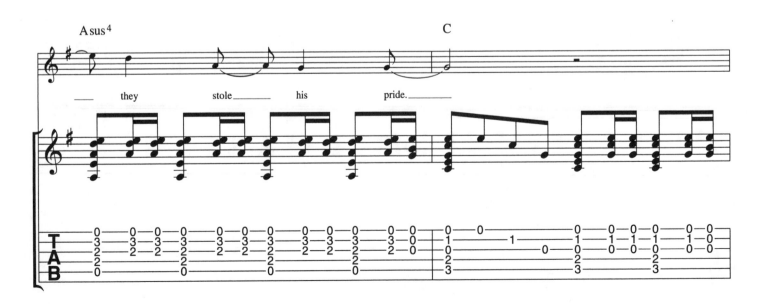

___ they stole___ his pride.___

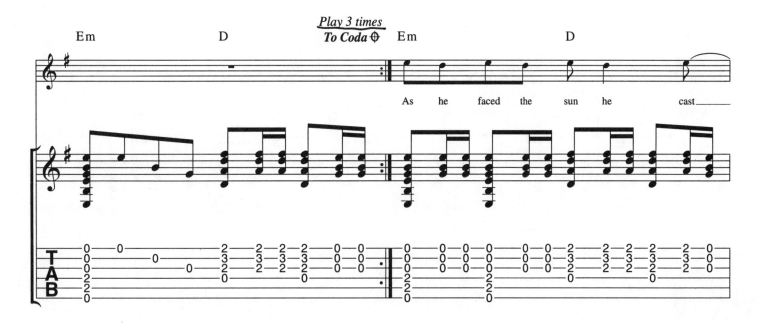

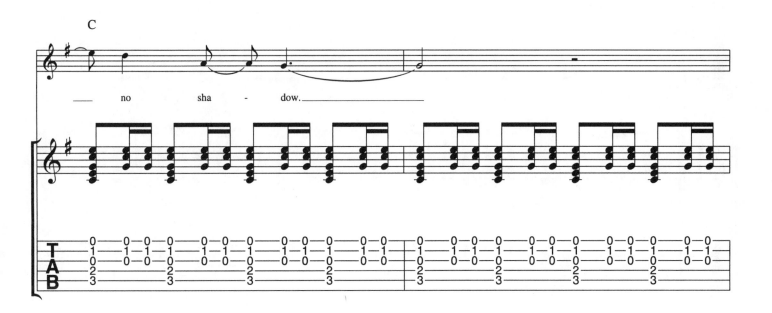

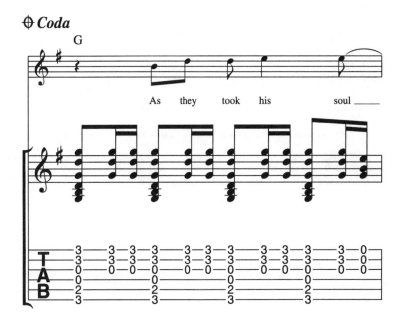

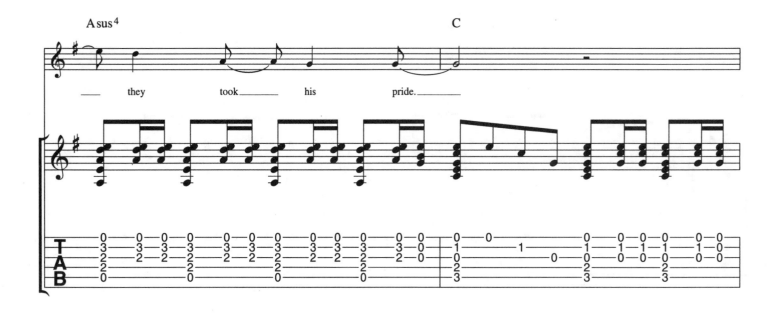

they took his pride.

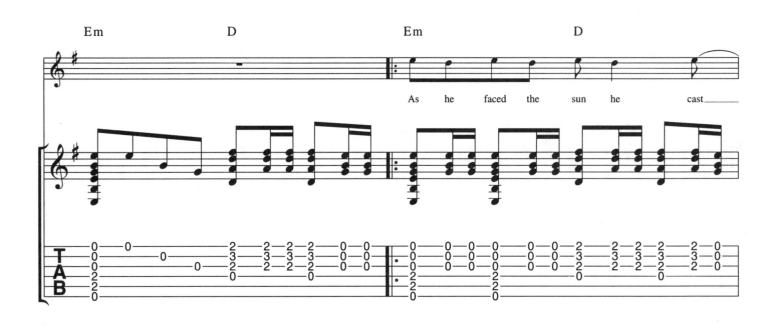

As he faced the sun he cast

1,2,3.

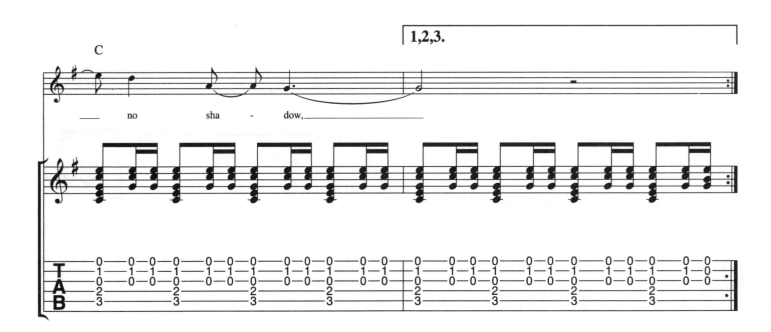

no sha - dow,

46

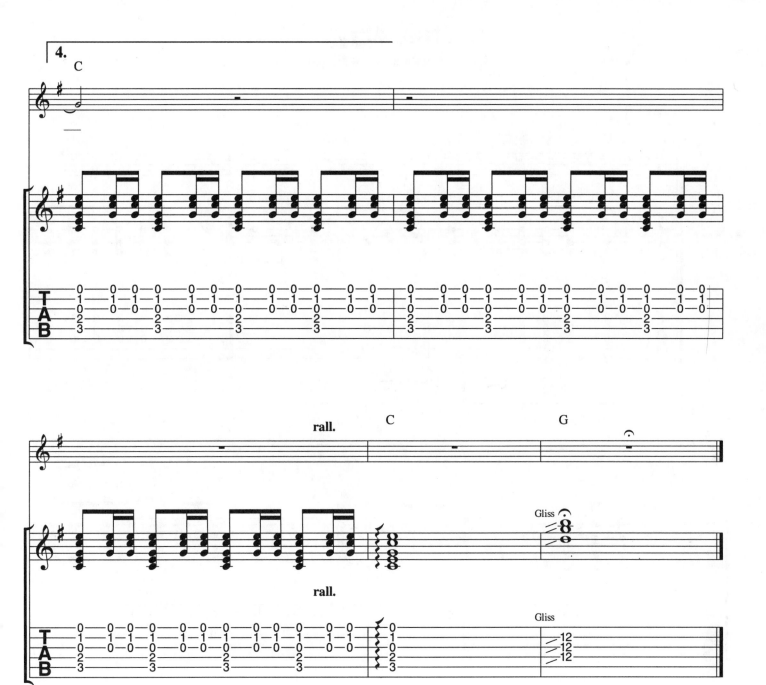

Hey Now

Words & Music by Noel Gallagher

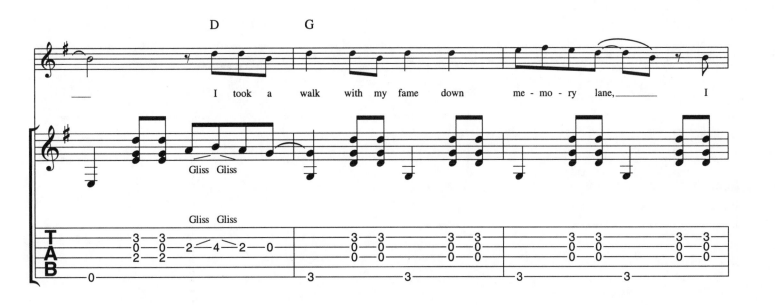

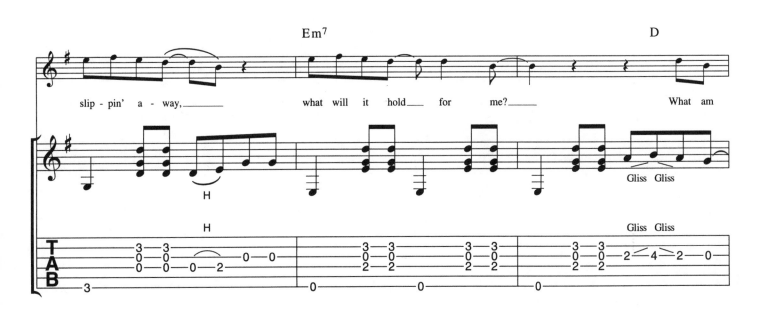

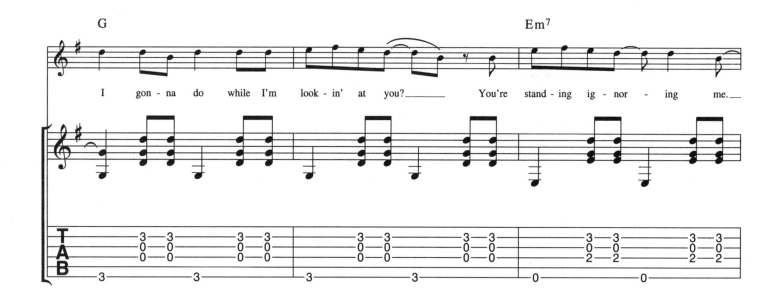

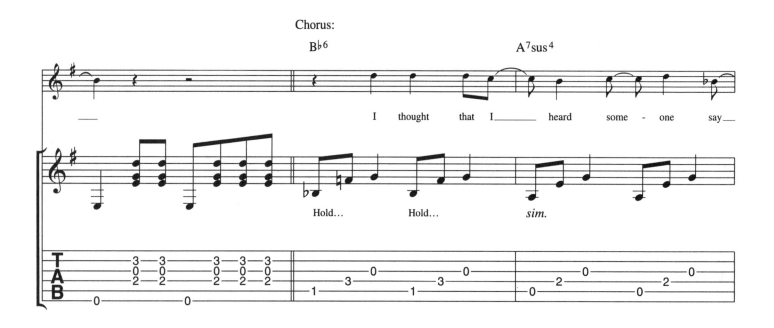

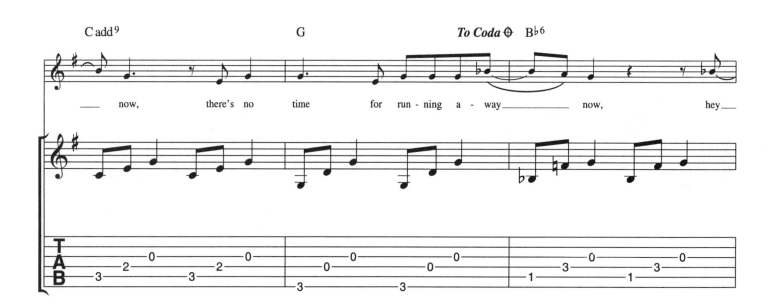

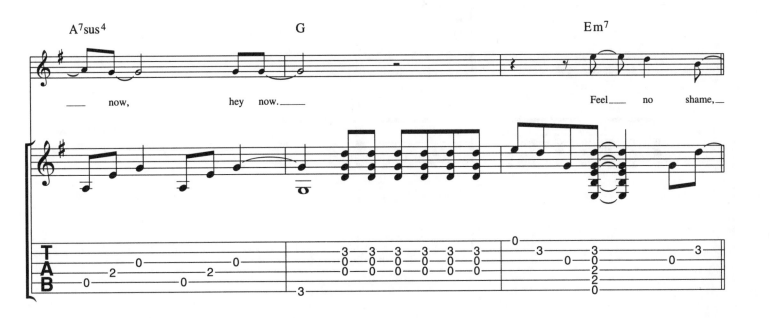

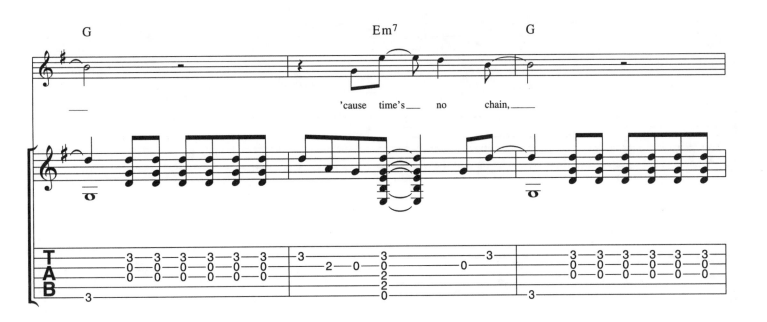

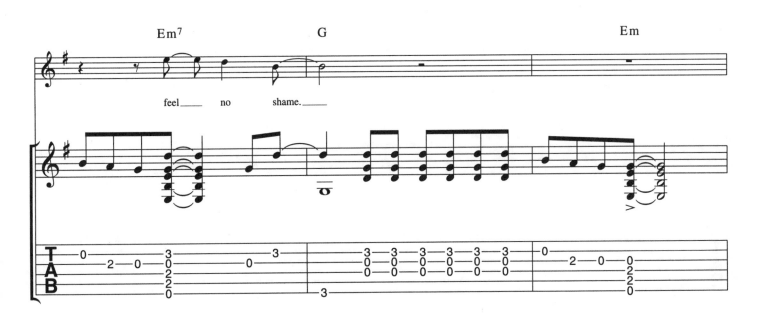

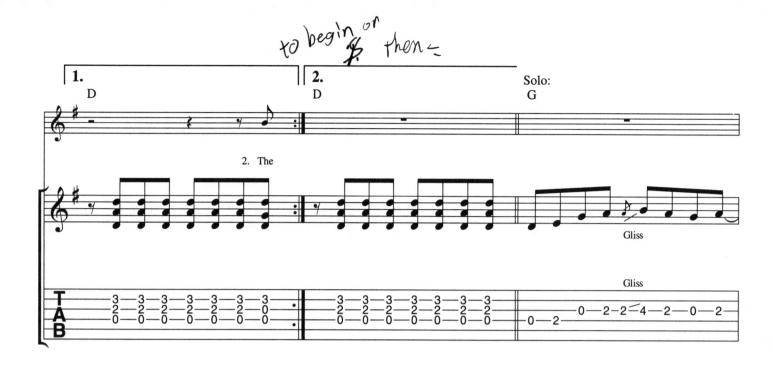

to begin or then —

1. D

2. D   Solo: G

2. The

Gliss

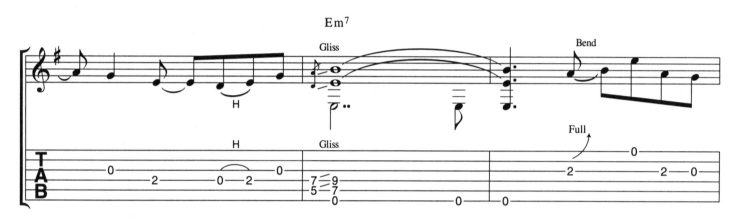

Em⁷

Gliss   Bend

H   Gliss   Full

G   Em⁷

Gliss   Gliss

B♭⁶   A⁷sus⁴   C add⁹

Bend   ½

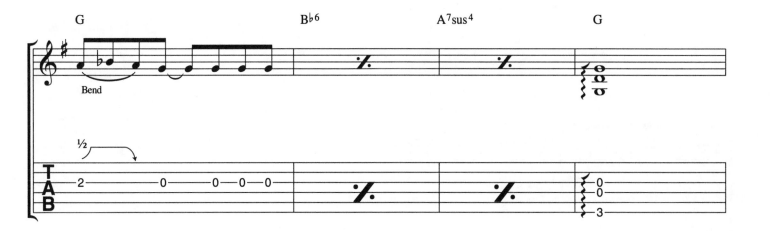

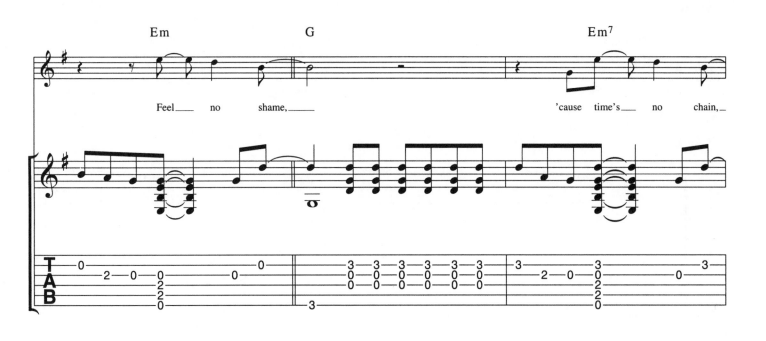

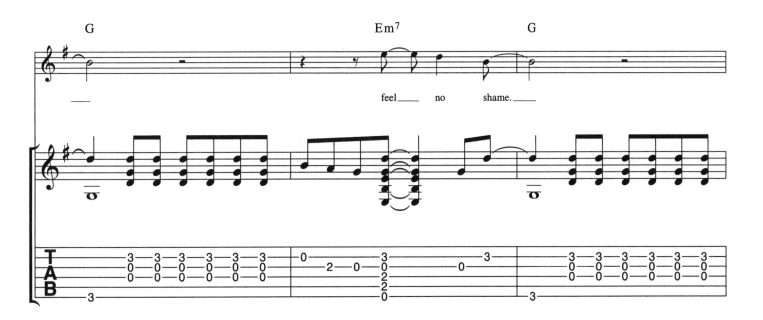

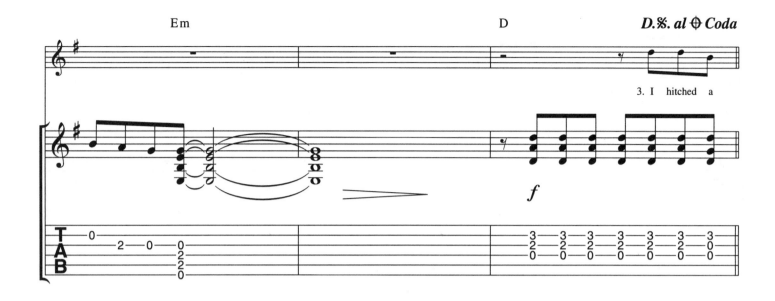

3. I hitched a

Coda ⊕

now,＿＿ hey＿＿ now,＿＿ hey＿＿

Hold...＿＿ sim.

now,＿＿ hey＿＿ now. Hey＿＿ now,＿＿ hey＿＿

Verse 2:

The first thing I saw
As I walked through the door
Was a sign on the wall that read
It said you might never know
That I want you to know
What's written inside of your head.

And time as it stands
Won't be held in my hands
Or living inside of my skin
And as it fell from the sky
I asked myself why
Can I never let anyone in?

The Swamp Song

Words & Music by Noel Gallagher

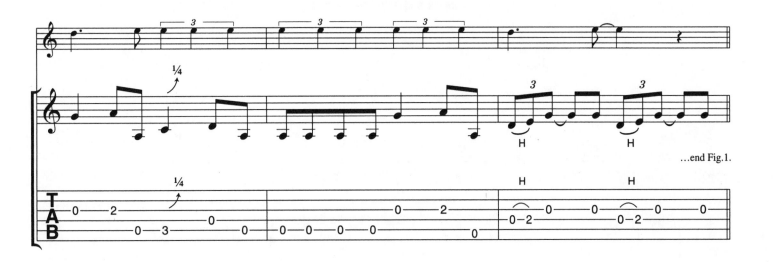

...end Fig.1.

Solo:

Am

Rhythm gtr continues Fig.1

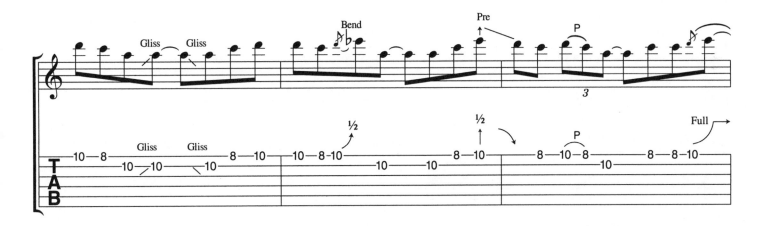

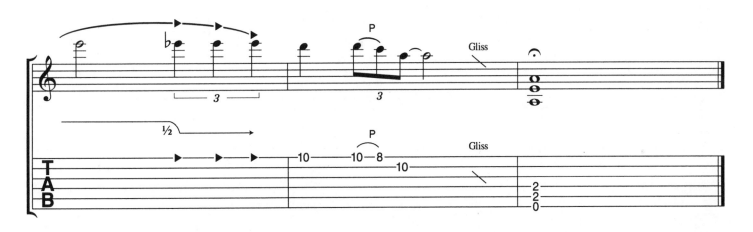

Some Might Say

Words & Music by Noel Gallagher

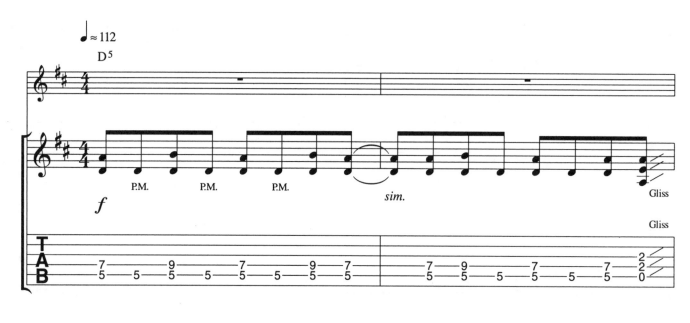

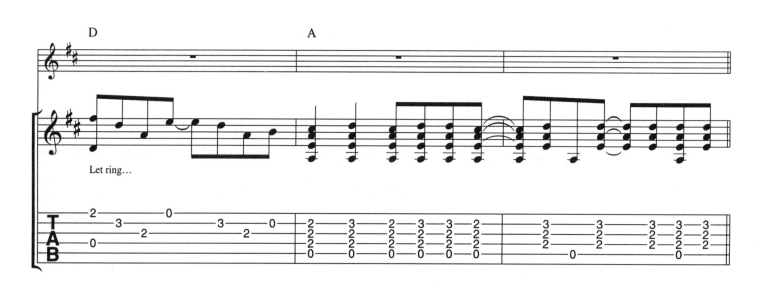

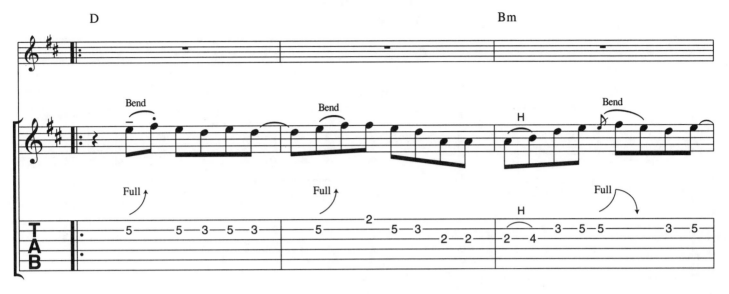

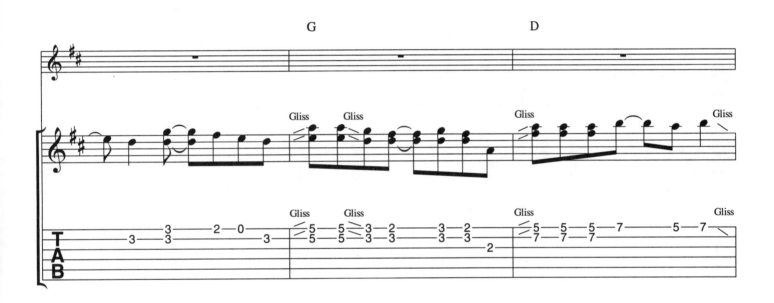

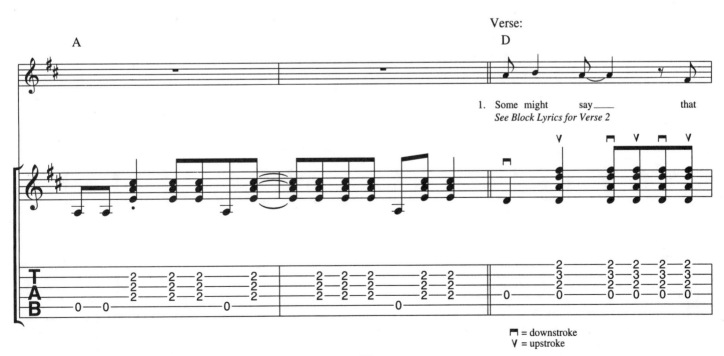

1. Some might say___ that
See Block Lyrics for Verse 2

⊓ = downstroke
V = upstroke

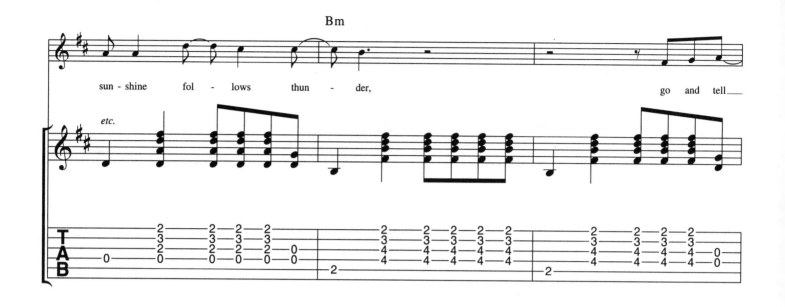

sun - shine fol - lows thun - der, go and tell___

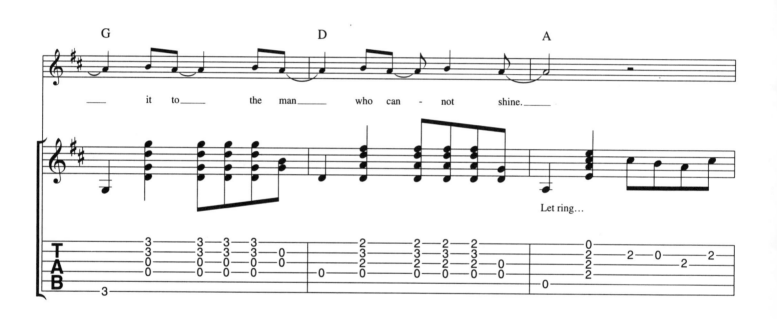

___ it to___ the man___ who can - not shine.___

Let ring…

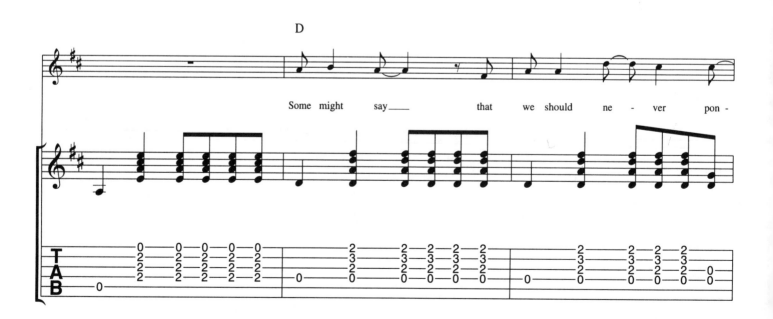

Some might say___ that we should ne - ver pon -

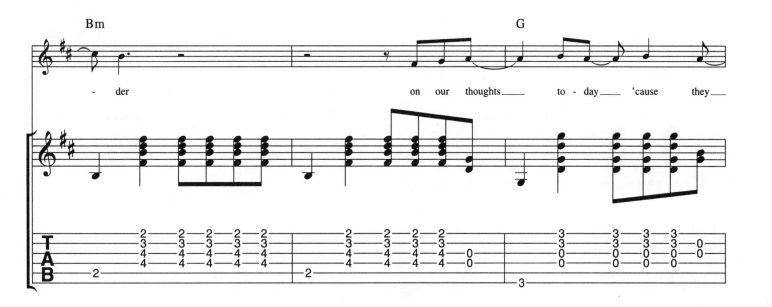

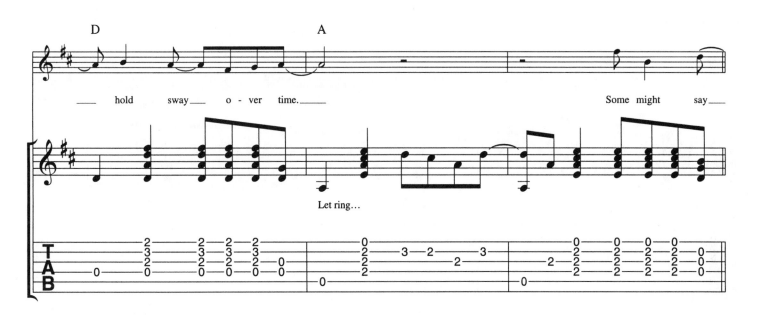

Chorus:

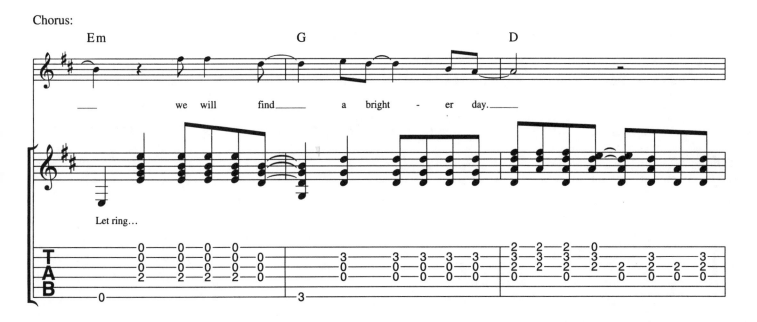

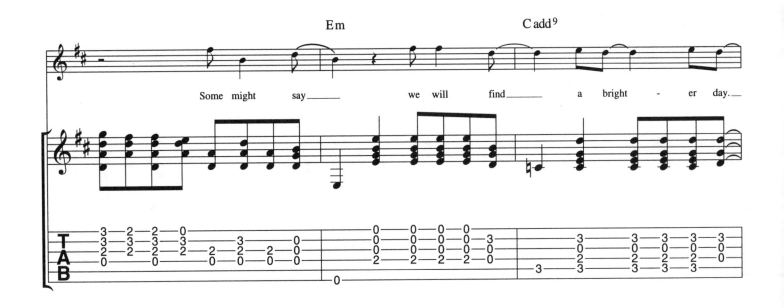

Some might say_____ we will find_____ a bright - er day._____

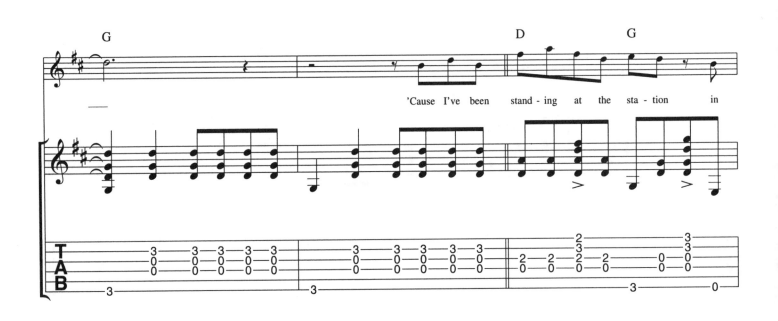

'Cause I've been stand - ing at the sta - tion in

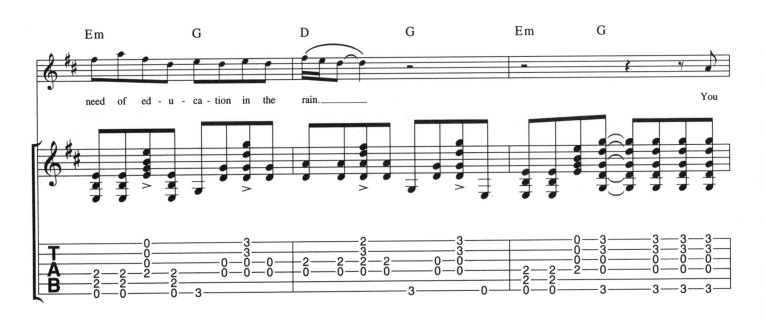

need of ed - u - ca - tion in the rain._____ You

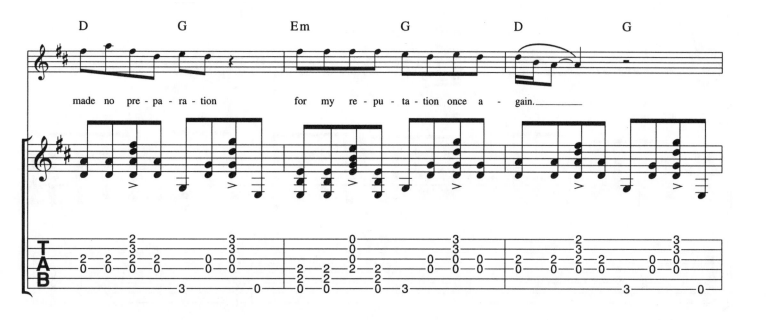

made no pre - pa - ra - tion   for my re - pu - ta - tion once a - gain.____

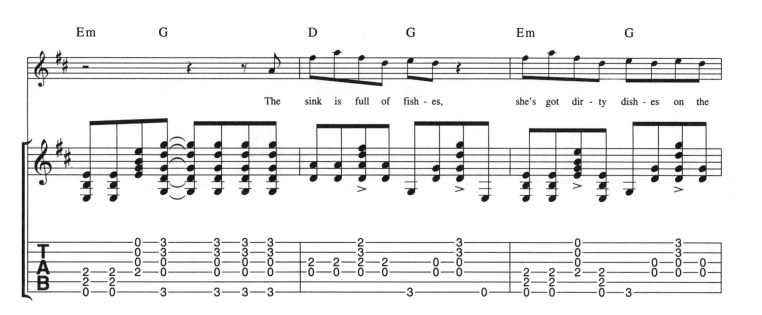

The sink is full of fish - es,   she's got dir - ty dish - es on the

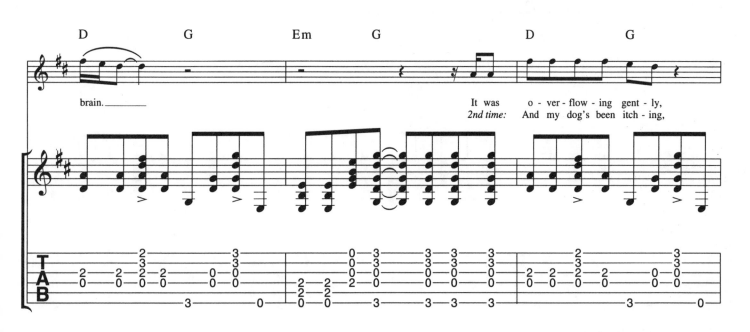

brain.____

It was   o - ver - flow - ing gent - ly,
2nd time: And my dog's been itch - ing,

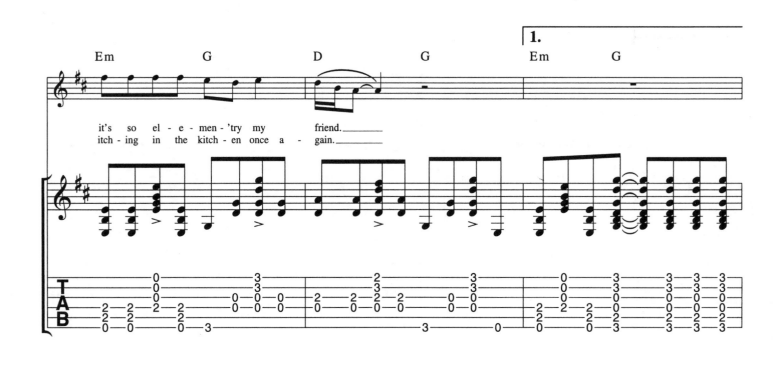

it's so el - e - men - 'try my   friend._____
itch - ing in the kitch - en once a - gain._____

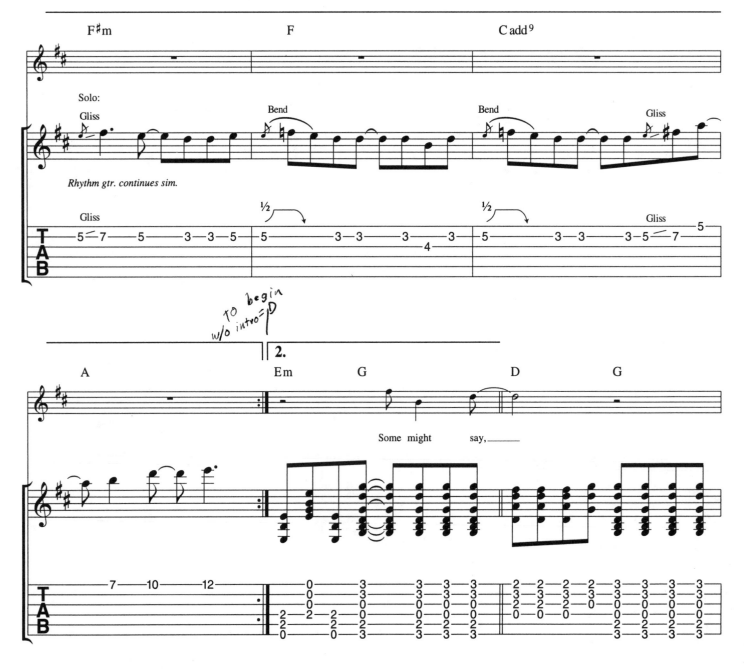

Solo:

Rhythm gtr. continues sim.

TO begin
w/o intro =

Some might   say,_____

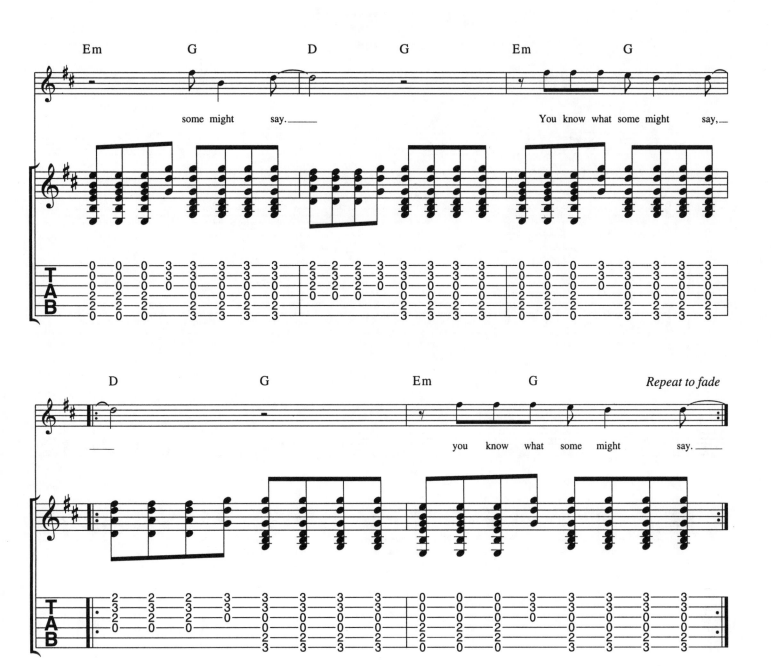

Verse 2:
Some might say they don't believe in heaven
Go and tell it to the man who lives in hell
Some might say you get what you've been given
If you don't get yours I won't get mine as well.

She's Electric

Words & Music by Noel Gallagher

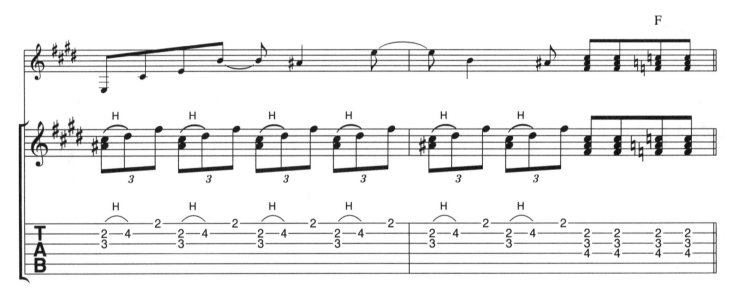

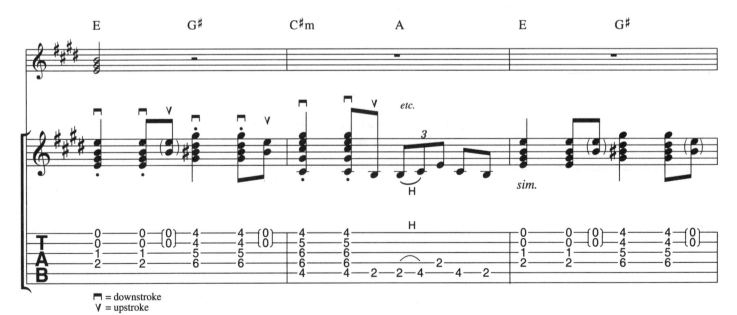

⊓ = downstroke
V = upstroke

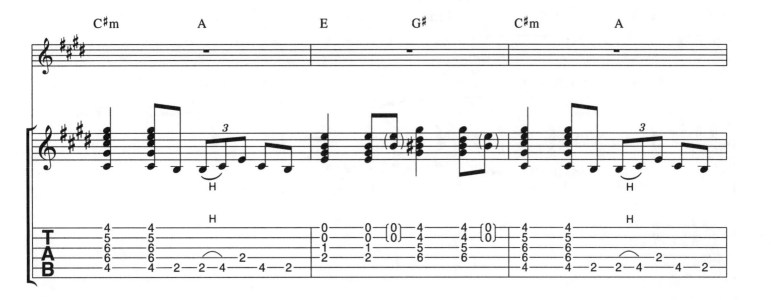

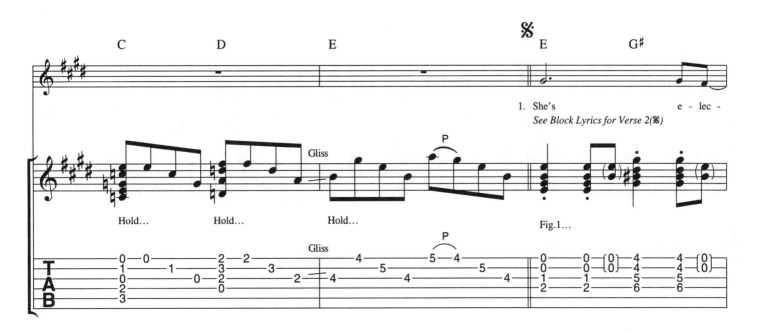

1. She's e - lec -
See Block Lyrics for Verse 2(%)

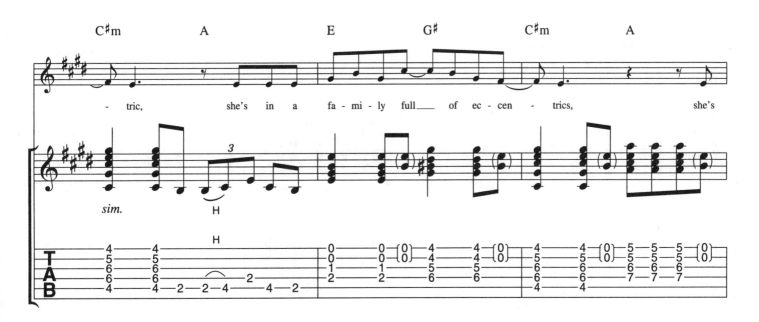

- tric, she's in a fa - mi - ly full___ of ec - cen - trics, she's

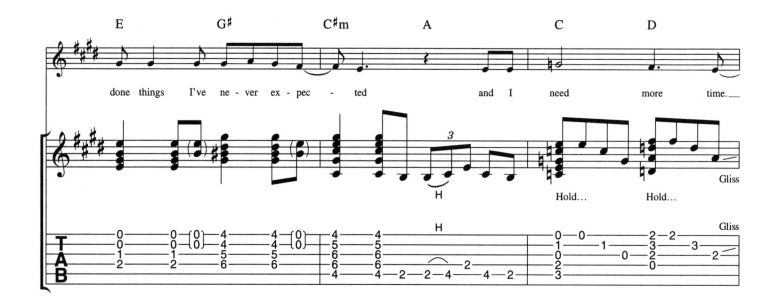

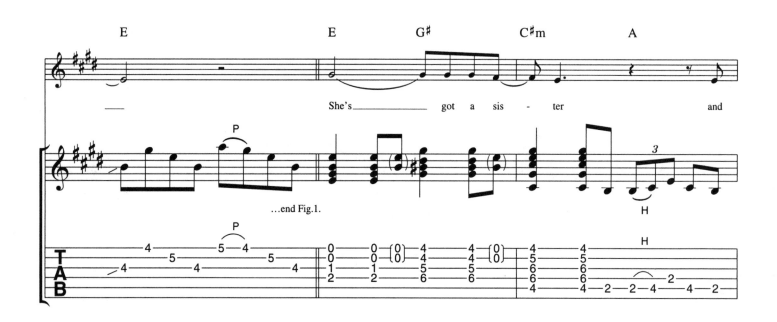

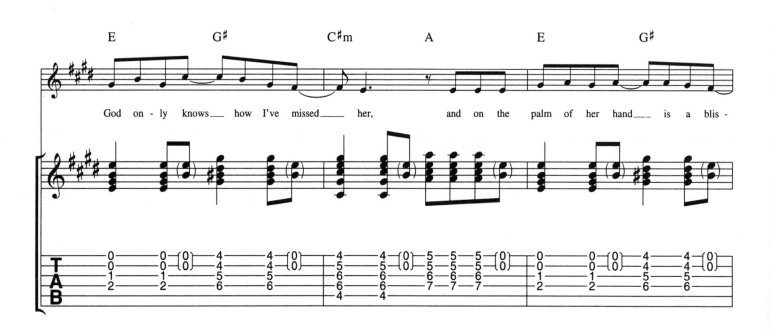

68

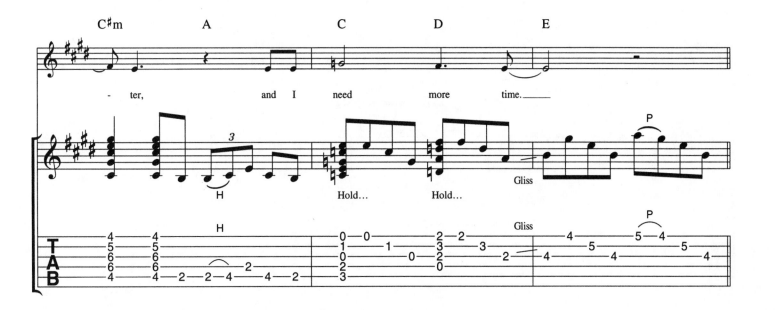

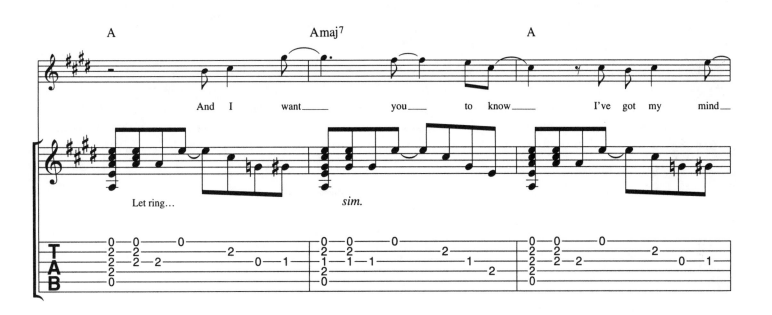

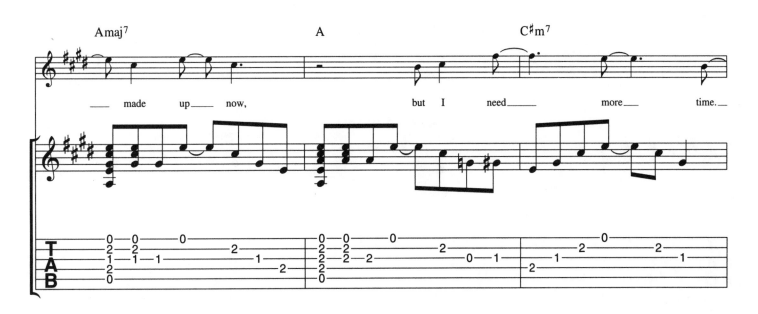

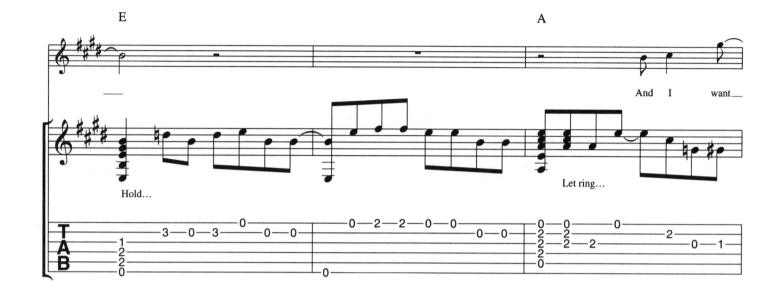

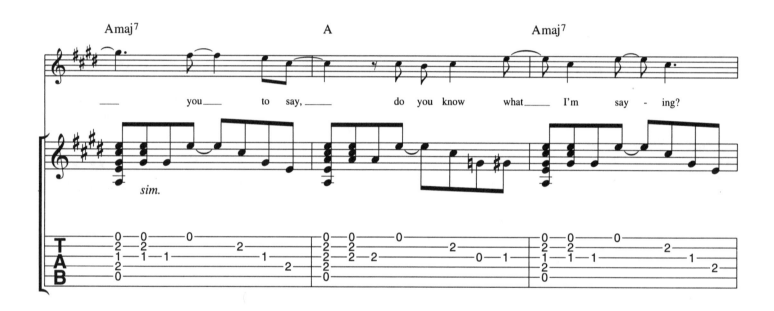

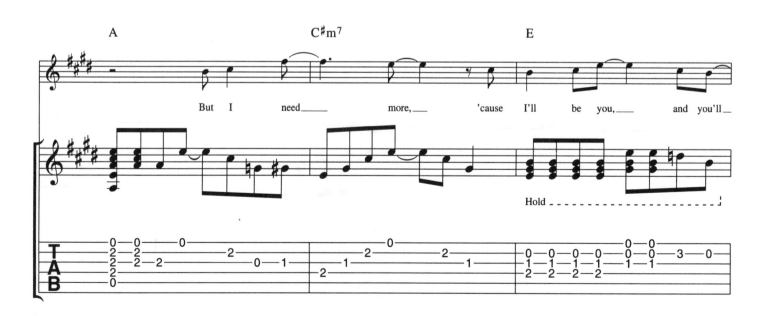

70

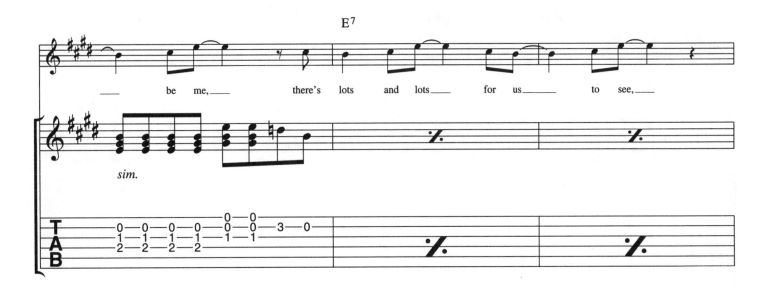

be me,____ there's lots and lots____ for us____ to see,____

sim.

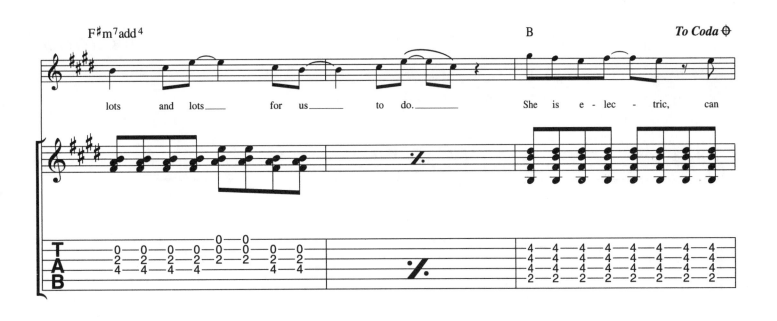

F#m7add4

B

To Coda ⊕

lots and lots____ for us____ to do.____ She is e - lec - tric, can

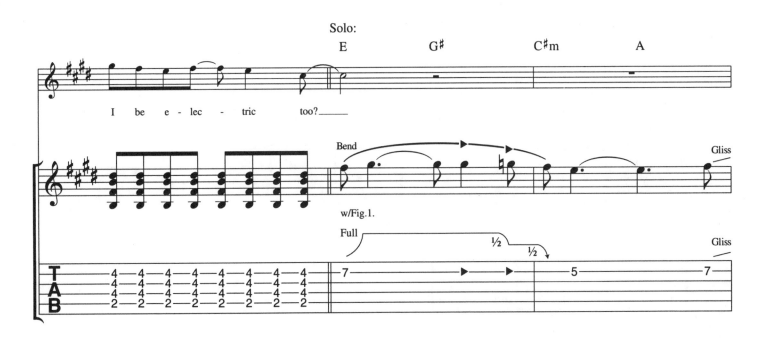

Solo:

E   G#   C#m   A

I be e - lec - tric too?____

Bend

w/Fig.1.

Gliss

Full   ½   ½

Gliss

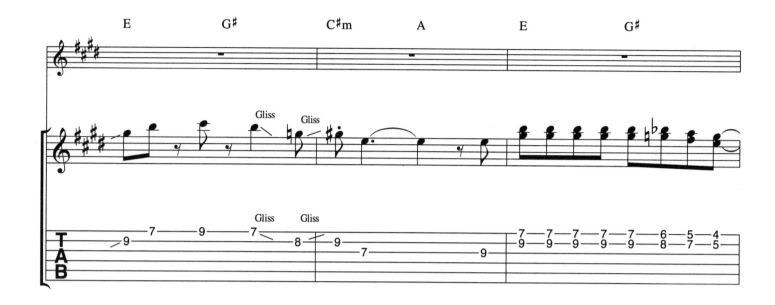

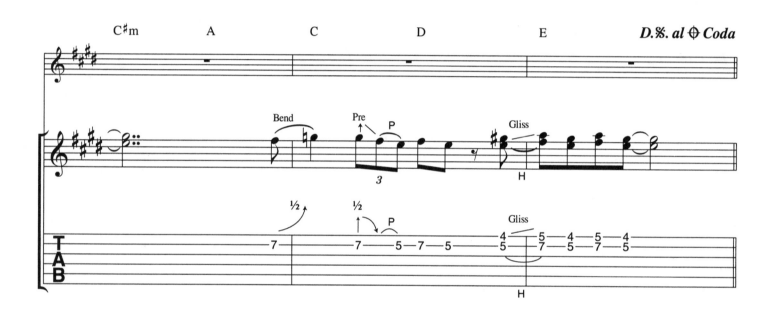

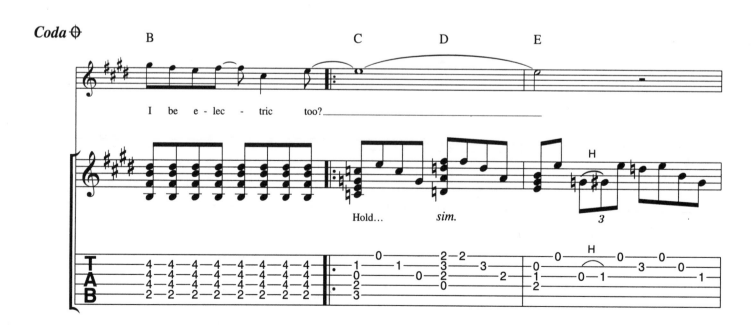

I be e-lec-tric too?

72

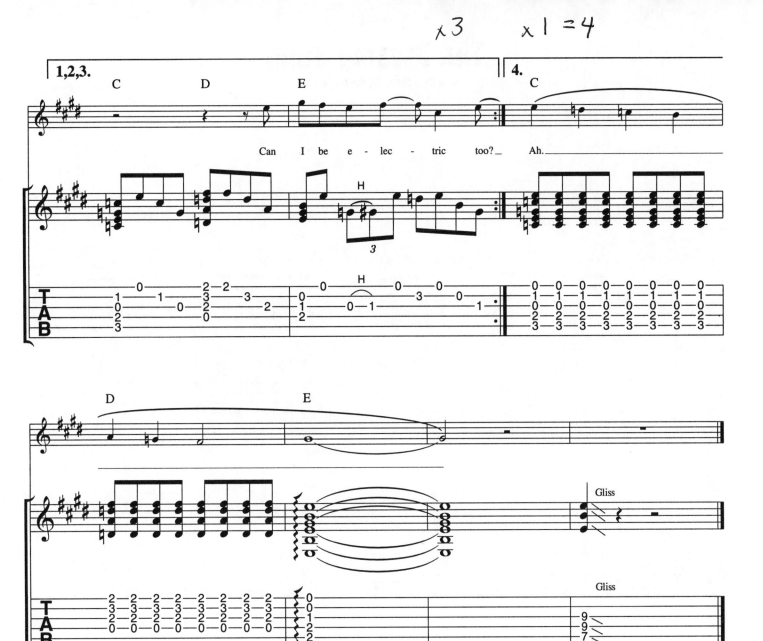

Verse 2(%):
She's got a brother
We don't get on with one another
But I quite fancy her mother
And I think that she likes me
She's got a cousin
In fact she's got 'bout a dozen
She's got one in the oven
But it's nothing to do with me.

The Swamp Song

Words & Music by Noel Gallagher

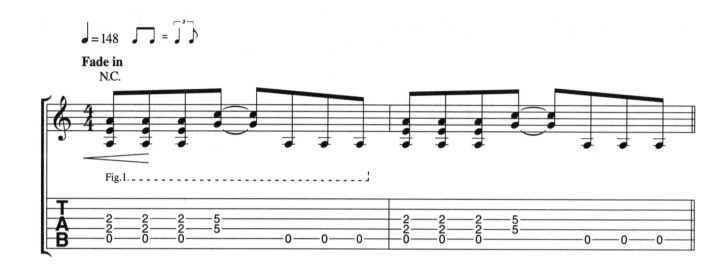

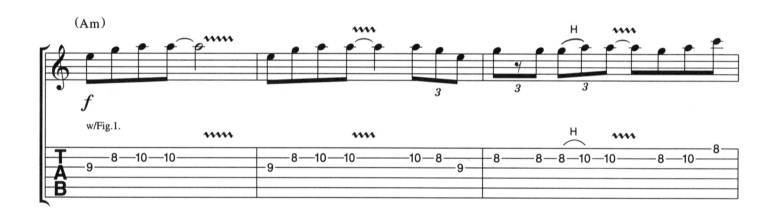

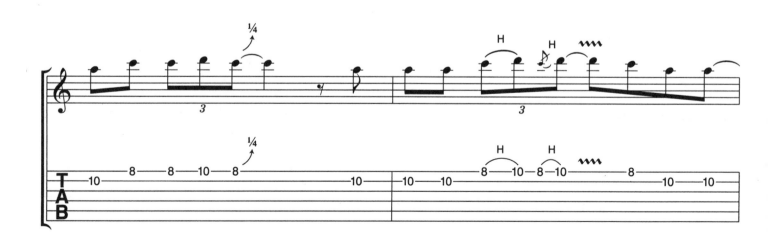

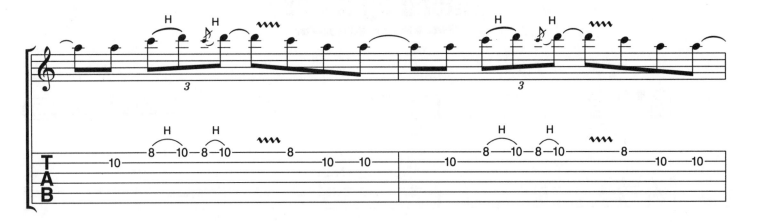

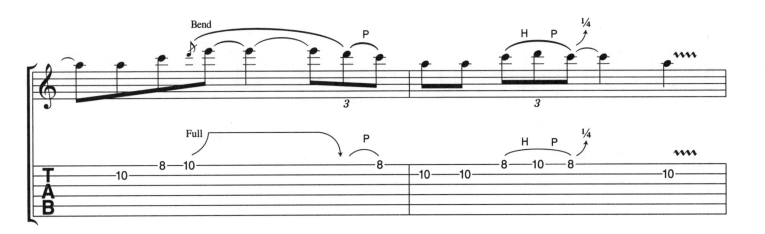

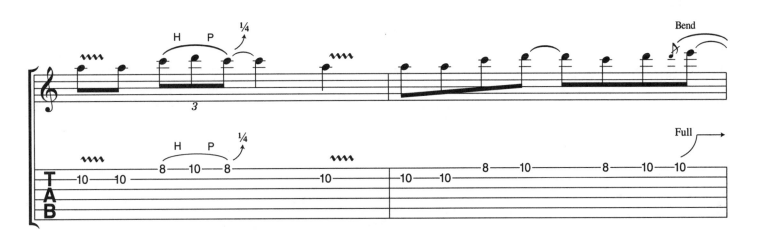

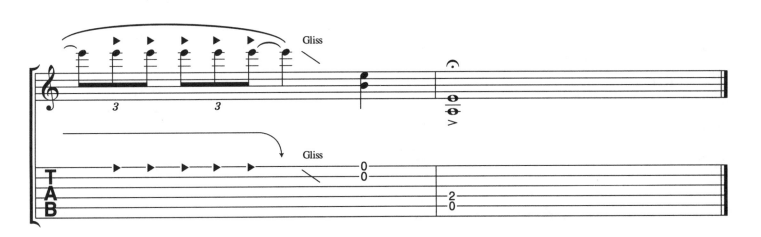

Morning Glory

Words & Music by Noel Gallagher

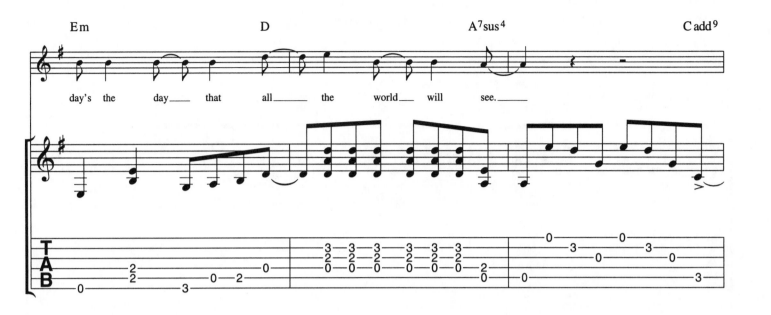

day's the day___ that all___ the world___ will see.___

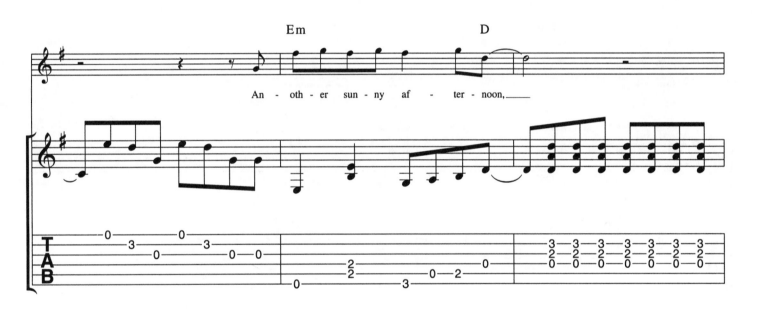

An - oth - er sun - ny af - ter - noon,___

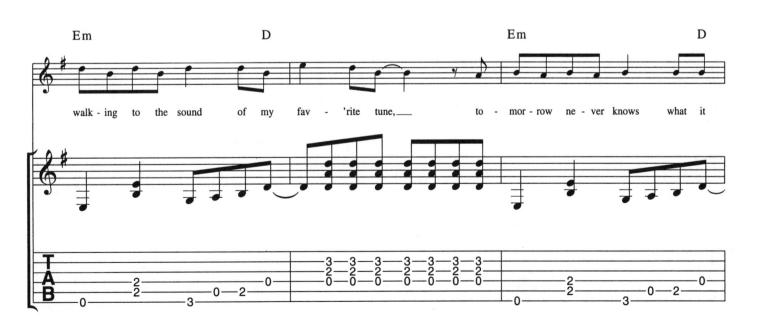

walk - ing to the sound of my fav - 'rite tune,___ to - mor - row ne - ver knows what it

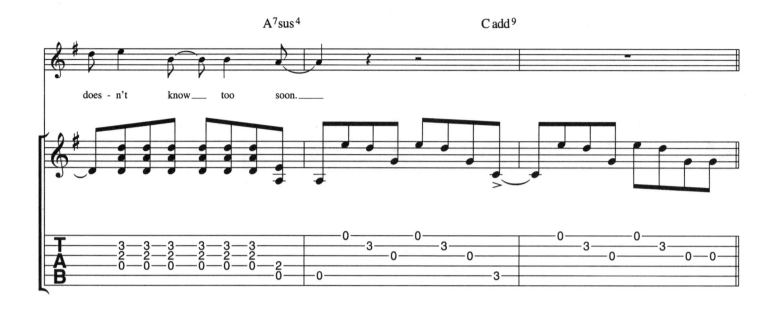

does-n't know____ too soon.____

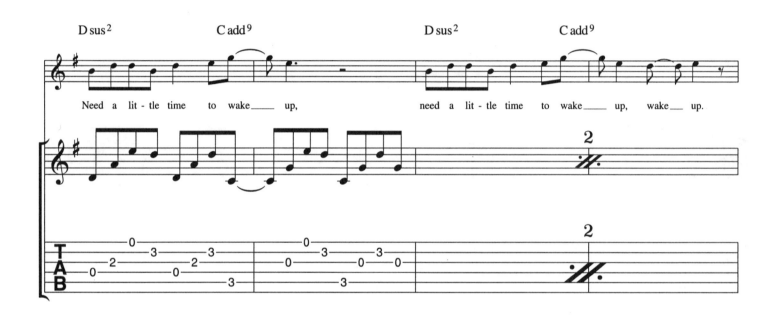

Need a lit-tle time to wake____ up, need a lit-tle time to wake____ up, wake____ up.

Need a lit-tle time to wake____ up, need a lit-tle time to rest____ your mind,____ you

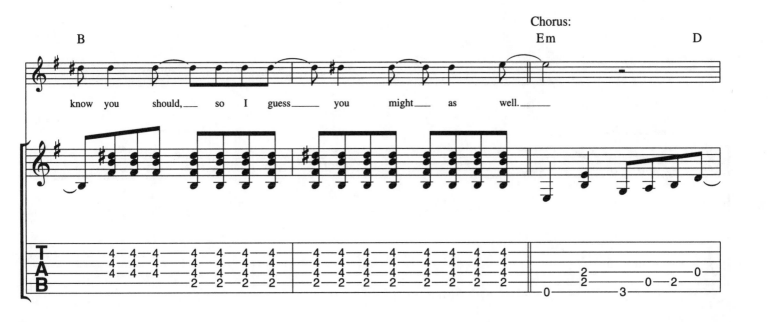

know you should,___ so I guess___ you might___ as well.___

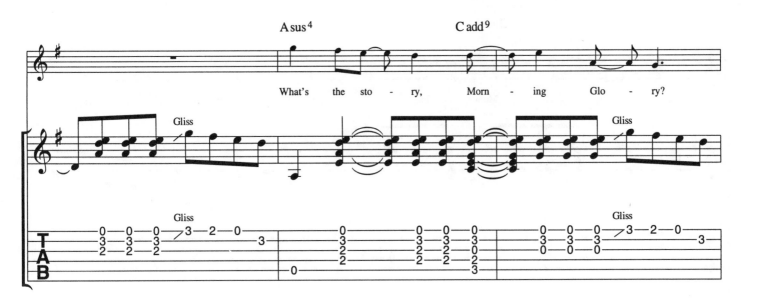

What's the sto - ry, Morn - ing Glo - ry?

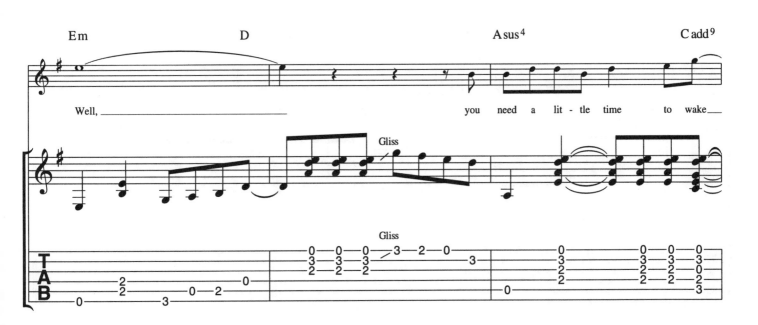

Well,_____ you need a lit - tle time to wake___

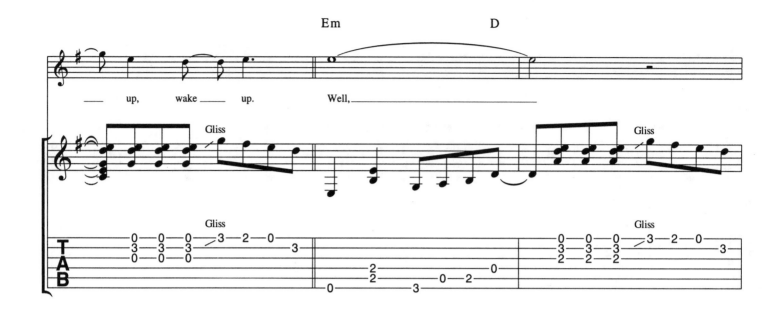

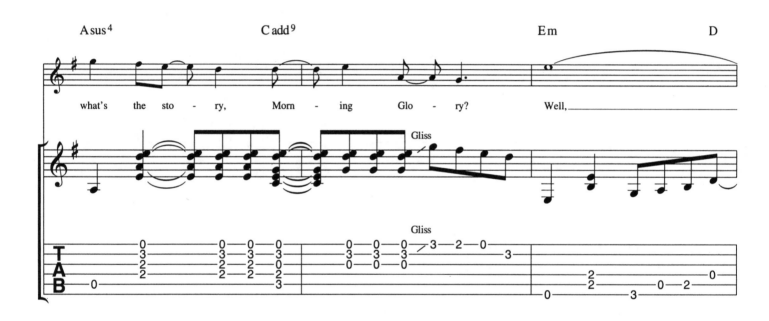

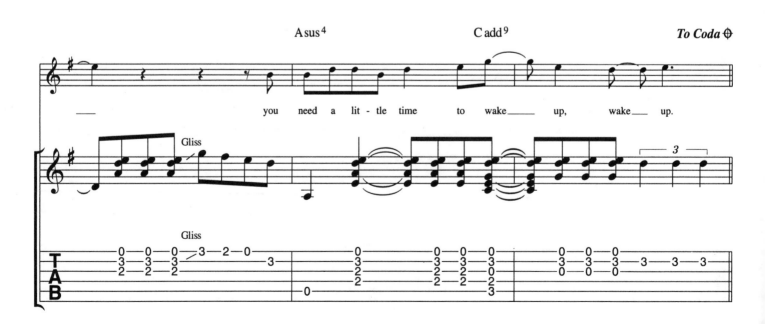

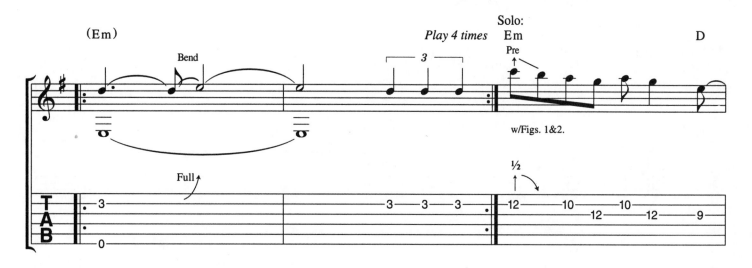

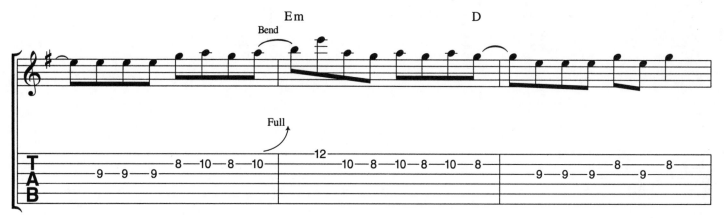

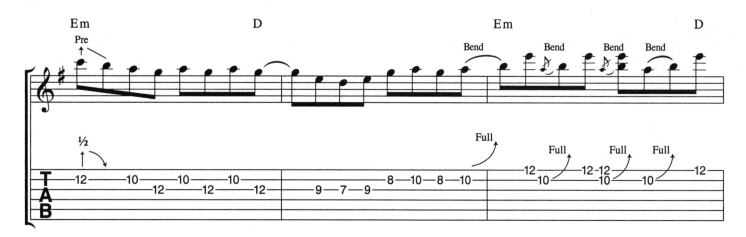

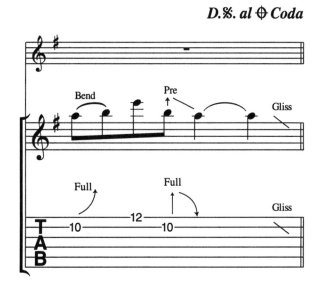

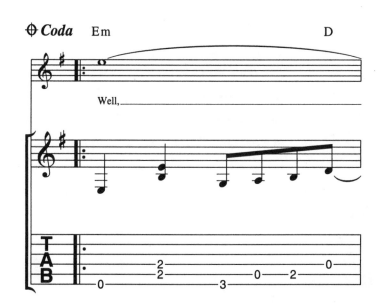

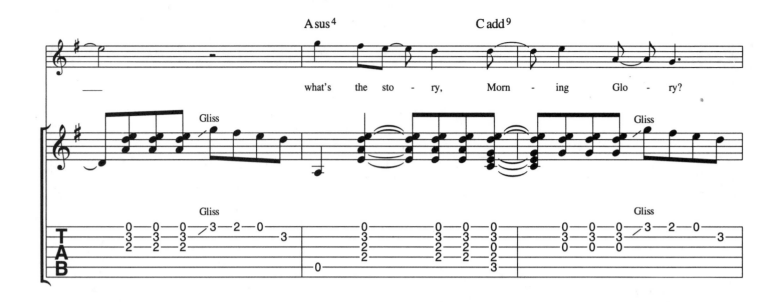

what's the sto - ry, Morn - ing Glo - ry?

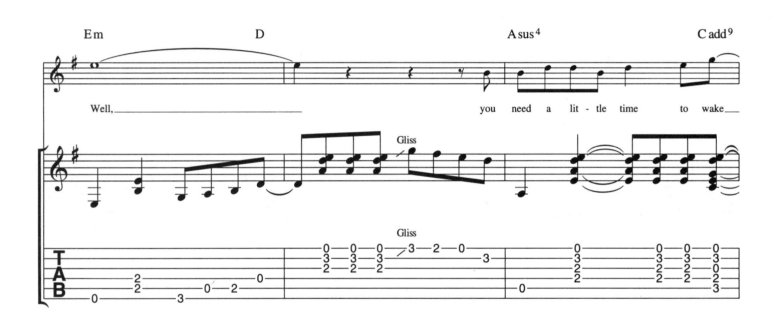

Well, _____ you need a lit - tle time to wake ___

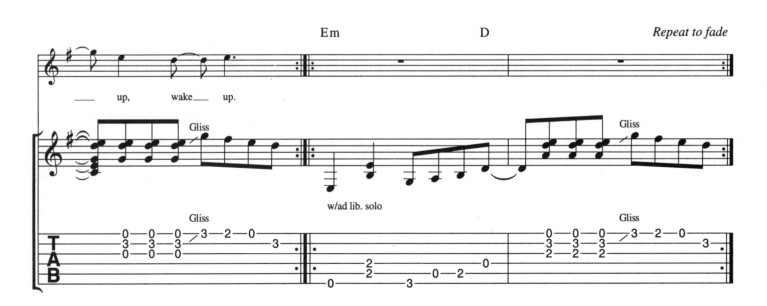

___ up, wake __ up.

Repeat to fade

w/ad lib. solo

Champagne Supernova

Words & Music by Noel Gallagher

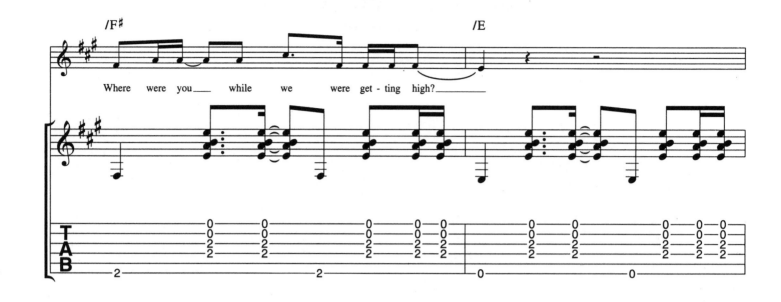

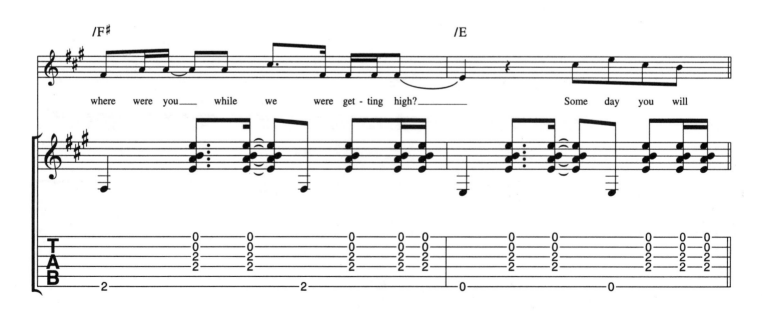

Chorus:

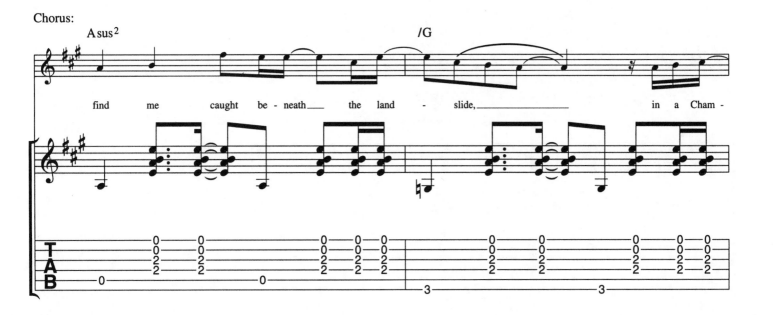

find me caught be - neath___ the land - slide,_____ in a Cham -

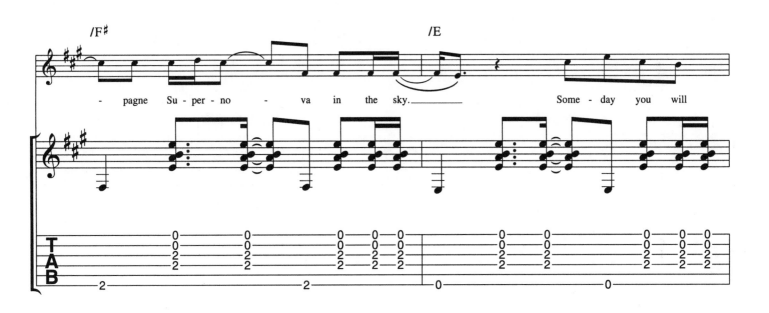

- pagne Su - per - no - va in the sky._____ Some - day you will

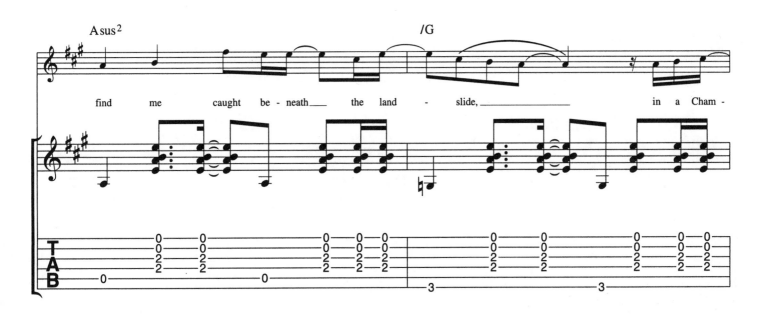

find me caught be - neath___ the land - slide,_____ in a Cham -

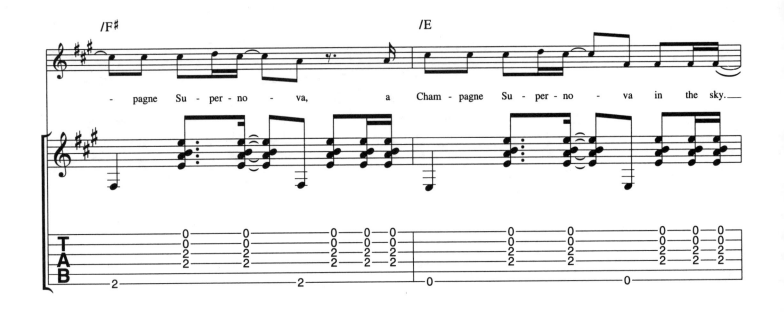

-pagne Su - per - no - va,   a Cham - pagne Su - per - no - va in the sky.

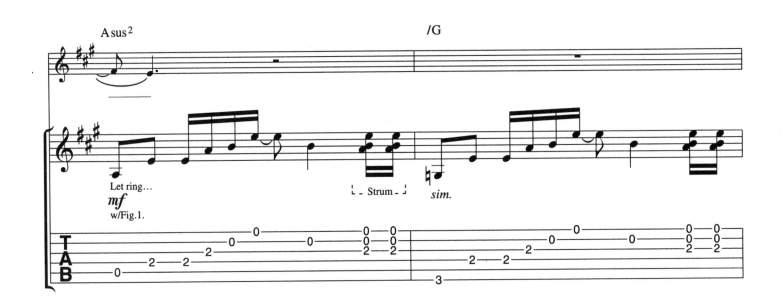

Let ring...
mf
w/Fig.1.

Strum

sim.

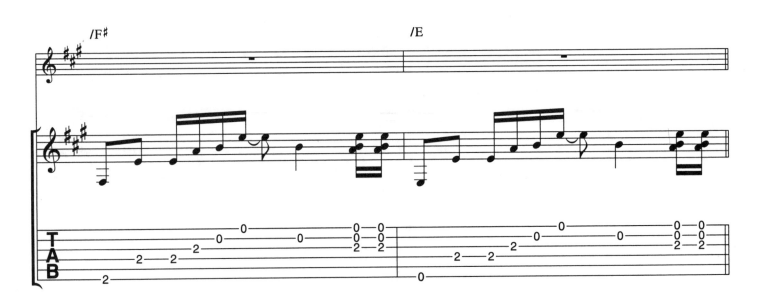

Go to here, E before Na's

Verse:

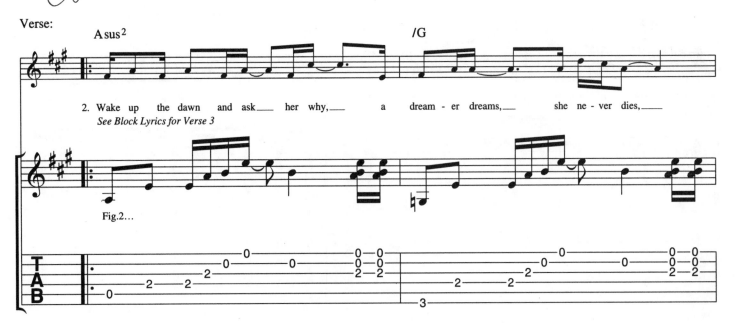

2. Wake up the dawn and ask____ her why,____ a dream - er dreams,____ she ne - ver dies,____
See Block Lyrics for Verse 3

Fig.2…

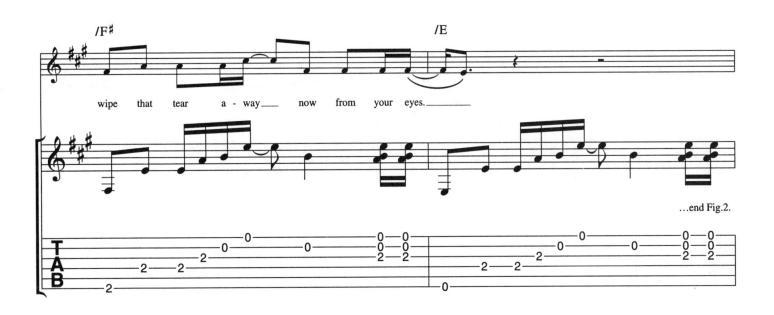

wipe that tear a - way____ now from your eyes.____

…end Fig.2.

Slow - ly walk - in' down____ the hall,____ fast - er than____ a can - non ball,____

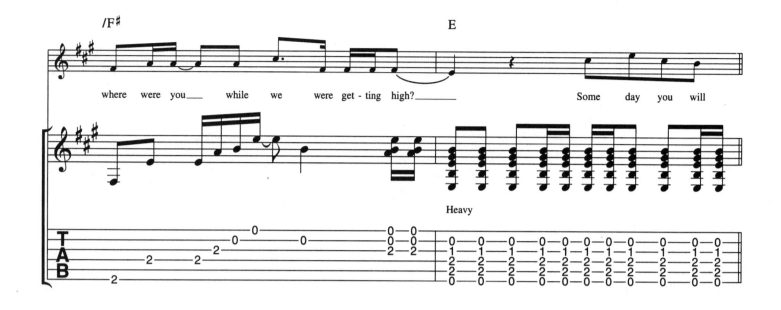

where were you___ while we were get-ting high?___ Some day you will

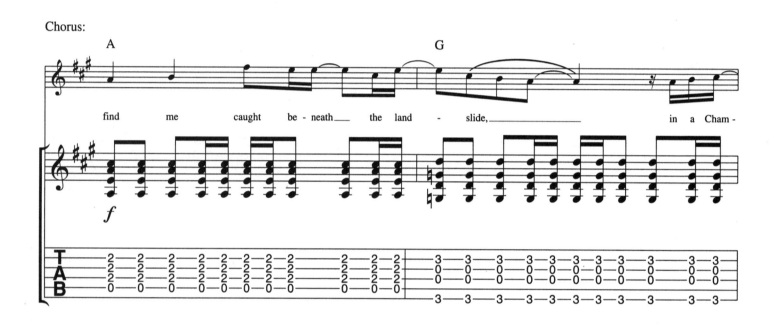

Chorus:

find me caught be-neath___ the land - slide,_____ in a Cham-

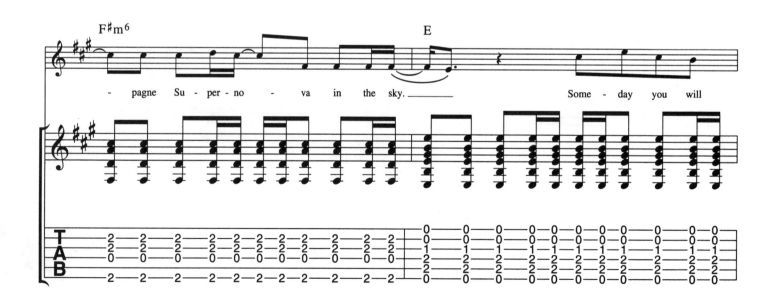

-pagne Su - per - no - va in the sky. ___ Some - day you will

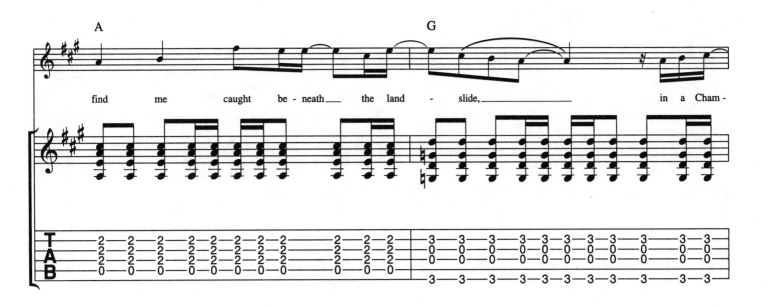

find me caught be - neath___ the land - slide,_____ in a Cham -

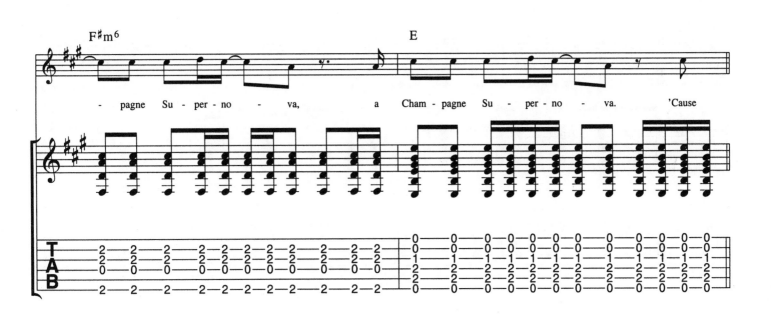

- pagne Su - per - no - va, a Cham - pagne Su - per - no - va. 'Cause

Bridge:

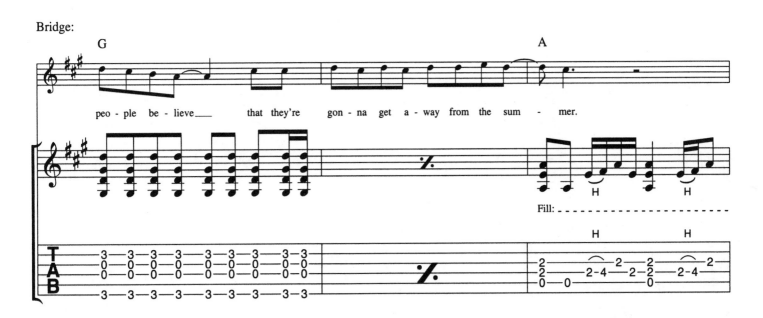

peo - ple be - lieve___ that they're gon - na get a - way from the sum - mer.

But you and I,_____ we live and die,_____ the

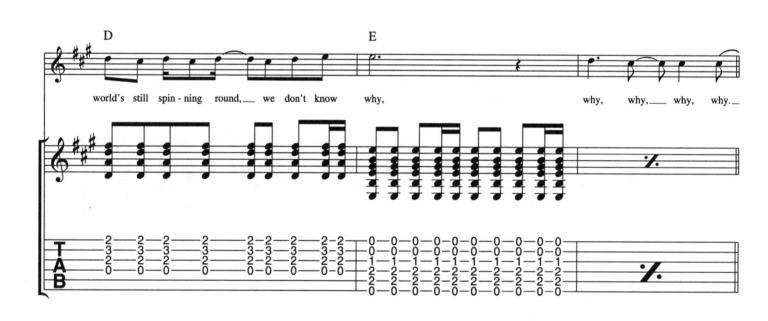

world's still spin - ning round,___ we don't know why,

why, why,___ why, why.___

1.

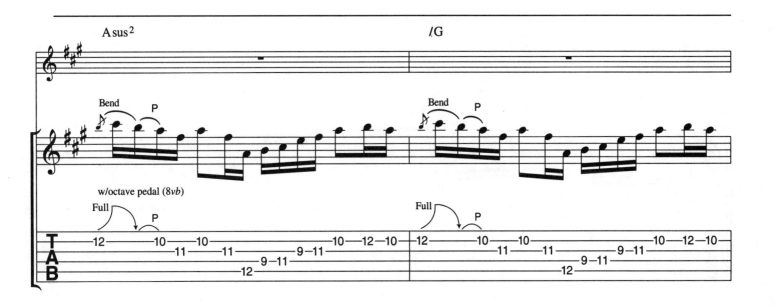

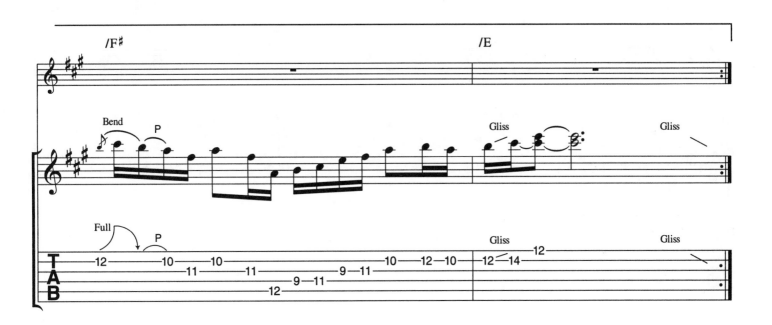

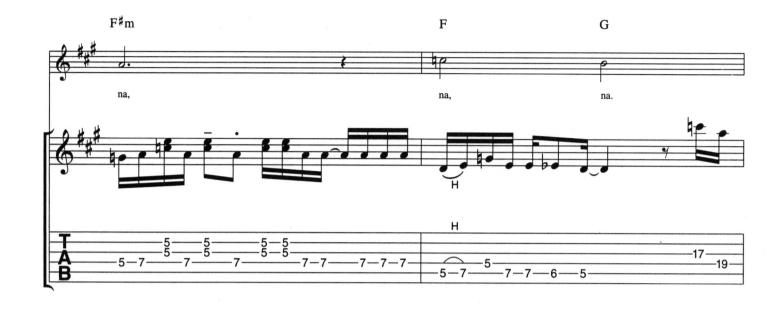

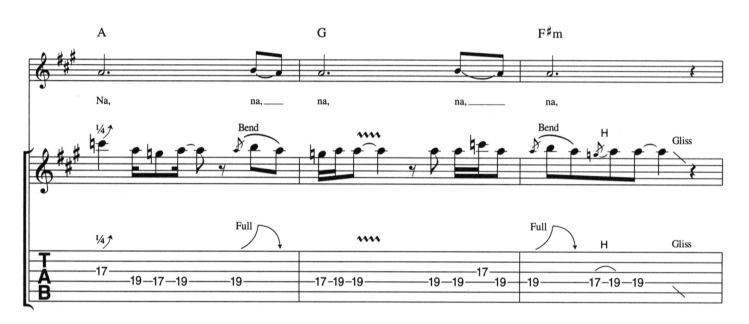

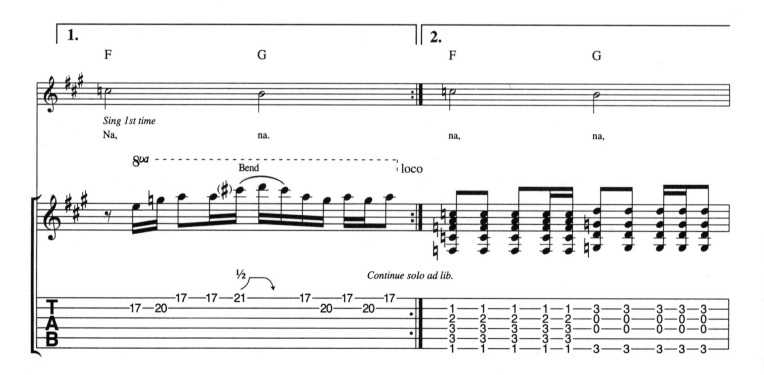

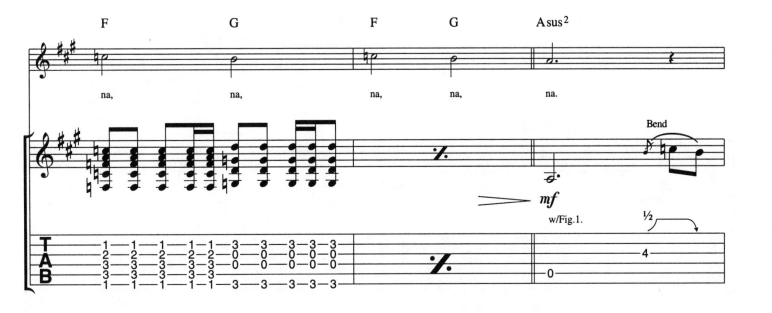

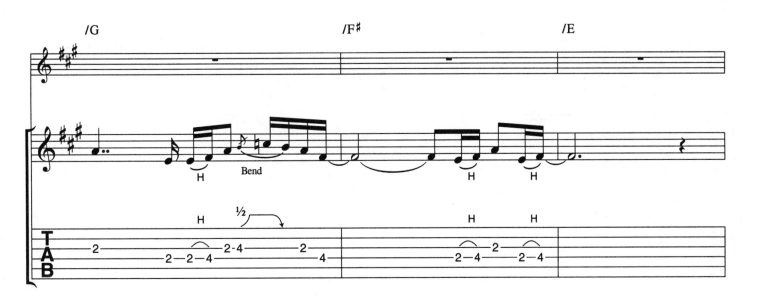

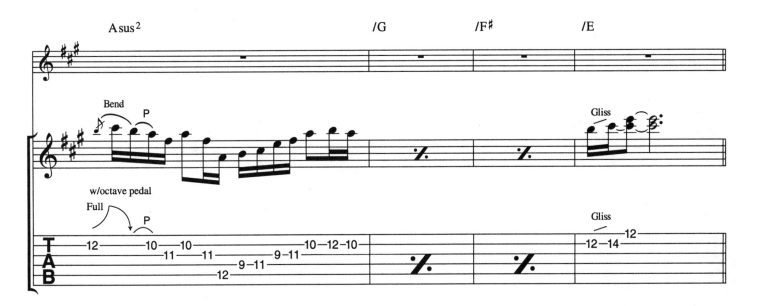

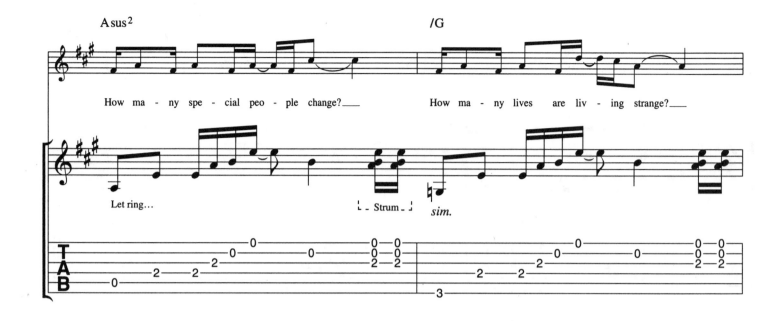

Asus²   /G

How ma - ny spe - cial peo - ple change?___ How ma - ny lives are liv - ing strange?___

Let ring…   Strum   sim.

/F#   /E

Where were you___ when we were get - ting high?___ We were get - ting high.___

end →

Asus²   /G

We were get - ting high,___ we were get - ting high,___

94

Verse 3:
How many special people change?
How many lives are living strange?
Where were you while we were getting high?
Slowly walkin' down the hall
Faster than a cannonball
Where were you while we were getting high?